Among the Peoples of the American West are these
multicultural schoolchildren of Central City, Colorado.
Courtesy of the Denver Public Library, Western History Department.

PEOPLES OF THE AMERICAN WEST:

historical perspectives through children's literature

by
MARY HURLBUT CORDIER
and
MARÍA A. PÉREZ-STABLE

The Scarecrow Press, Inc.
Metuchen, N.J., & London
1989

British Library Cataloguing-in-Publication data available

Library of Congress Cataloging-in-Publication Data

Cordier, Mary Hurlbut, 1930-
  Peoples of the American West.

  Includes bibliographical references and index.
  1. Children's literature, American--Bibliography. 2. West
(U.S.) in literature--Bibliography. 3. Western stories--
Bibliography. 4. History in literature--Bibliography. 5. Indi-
ans in literature--Bibliography. 6. Frontier and pioneer life in
literature--Bibliography. 7. Overland journeys to the Pacific in
literature--Bibliography. 8. Children--Books and reading.
I. Pérez-Stable, María A. II. Title.
Z1037.C8 1989   011.62   89-10284
ISBN 0-8108-2240-7

This book is dedicated
to the real-life counterparts,
both historical and present-day,
of Lettie Ashmore, librarian
in *Eight Mules from Monterey,*
and schoolteacher Belle Warren
in *The Sodbuster Venture.*

TABLE OF CONTENTS

Grades: 4-9

Overland Journeys and Wagon Train Trips

Grades: K-3

Grades: 4-9

Immigration and the Immigrant Experience

Grades: K-3

Native Americans

Grades: K-3

American Southwest

West Coast

Acknowledgments

This project has been supported in part by grants from the College of Education and the Honors College of Western Michigan University for undergraduate student assistants Susan M. Bullock and Mary L. Knooihuisen. Their continuing interest and involvement beyond the terms of their grants are deeply appreciated and attests to their professional interest in elementary education. Ms. Bullock has also been instrumental in the final preparation of the book annotations.

The efficient staff of InterLibrary Loan Office, University Libraries, has made it possible for us to pursue this project by obtaining numerous books for review. Technical assistance in the preparation of the manuscript has been generously provided by Dr. Howard R. Poole and the staff of the Office of Instructional Development, and by the staff of the Merze Tate Research and Information Processing Center, Western Michigan University. Matthew B. Tisch has been the key person in the preparation of the manuscript for publication.

Our departments, Education and Professional Development and University Libraries, have encouraged our efforts in numerous ways. Special thanks to Dr. James W. Burns, Professor, Reading and Language Development, and the inservice elementary teachers in his graduate class in Reading Beyond the Basal Readers for assessing our proposed learning activities and the recommended books.

Mary Hurlbut Cordier   María A. Pérez-Stable
Associate Professor   Associate Professor
Education and Professional   University Libraries
    Development
                Western Michigan University
                  Kalamazoo, Michigan

Chapter One

An Introduction to Children's Historical Literature of the American West

Historical perspective for children is often simply the "olden days," the time and place beyond children's memories. The past often remains undifferentiated in children's thinking, or it takes on a crazy quilt chronology based on the lives and contributions of the "Great People" and the most prominent historical events. For many children, the history of the American West remains an intriguing mystery that may begin with Laura Ingalls' family in their "little house" somewhere near the frontier where there are Indians, settlers, outlaws, and soldiers. The "Little House" books represent appropriate and accessible slices of American social history with the Ingalls family as a sort of "Every White Man's" settler family. Through a broader examination of children's literature, both fiction and non-fiction, the lives of the multiracial, multiethnic peoples of the American West are also represented in appropriate settings with historical authenticity and with sympathetic character development. In this bibliography, *Peoples of the American West,* 100 historical fiction and other trade books for children have been selected that will expand and enrich children's historical understanding through the accessible lives of real people such as the Ingalls family, Elenore Plaisted, and Waheenee, and fictional but historically authentic characters such as Pie-Biter and Sarah "plain and tall."[1] Teachers, librarians and parents will surely add their own favorite children's literature about the American West to this list.

The task of developing multicultural and non-sexist perspectives of American western history is complicated by the persistence of the stereotypes of the people of the West. A reproducible worksheet for elementary children entitled, "The Best of West," identifies white male outlaws, cattlemen, several explorers, Calamity Jane, Belle Star, and a few Native American men, described mainly as warriors.[2] A publishing company has used a photograph in their advertisements for supplementary educational materials depicting a bulletin board map of the trails west, which, in this case, begin in Appalachia.[3] The trails, shown straight as a string, are lined with cut-outs of tipis and covered wagons implying the westward movement. While the accuracy of the map is open to question, it is the bulletin board list of "Pioneers" that most needs expansion. It includes white male explorers and Sacajawea as the token Native American and token woman. This type of instructional material stereotypes the people of the American West, and in doing so, excludes the historically authentic, multicultural women, men, and children in favor of a few notorious individuals and several notable men.

Elementary social studies textbooks, especially those published since the mid-1980s, broaden children's understanding of the multicultural heritage of the United States, including the West. In the later elementary textbooks, the content is rich with examples of the contributions of notable Americans from diverse origins. The famous-person approach to history highlights the heroes and heroines whom adults may identify as role models. For children, however, the mediation between the great people of history and their own lives may seem insurmountable. The great-person approach to history omits the overall picture in favor of a few significant people and events. Most children need more information and more experiential background in order to put the great people's lives into the flow of human events. Admittedly, the important people should be recognized, but in a balanced perspective that includes the ordinary but authentic people.

Children's literature can serve as the corollary to the social studies textbooks that provides this broadened and personalized perspective of the events of the past. In the process of reading "beyond the basal" social studies textbooks,[4] the factual content of history can come alive for children through the characters and the events portrayed. In order to aid teachers, librarians, parents, and children themselves in selecting children's historical fiction and non-fiction books that provide realism and understanding of the historical events of the American West, this *selective*, annotated bibliography of 100 books has been based on the following criteria:

1. **Realism of Time, Place, Events, and Characters.** The parameters set for inclusion in the bibliography are generally prior to 1900, and west of the Mississippi River within the contiguous United States. While the illustrations may be developed in a variety of styles and media, the pictures appropriately represent the characters, settings, and events. The characters portray many different ways of life, jobs, and conditions within the time frame and the environmental setting. The authentic portrayal of the time, place, events, and characters is essential in order to develop historical perspectives through children's literature.[5]

2. **Literary Qualities Based in a Good Story Line**. Characters are well-developed, and suitable to the time, place, and occurrences. Language, vocabulary, and actions are appropriate to the characters and the setting. Within the historical settings, the story line involves realistic human conflicts and problems, joys and sorrows, successes and failures, loves and hates.

3. **Availability of the Books.** All books included in the bibliography are in print or are widely available in school, public, or academic libraries as indicated by the Online Computer Library Center, Inc. (OCLC). Because the books are widely available, they can be acquired via Interlibrary Loan through school, public, and college libraries.

The criterion of realism is the foundation for the selection of children's literature in this bibliography. Through realistic historical fiction, children will learn that people much like themselves were the community builders, the planners and dreamers, and the protagonists in the actual drama of the West. To bring these multicultural people to life within the boundaries of historical accuracy will illustrate how people, their occupations, customs, and interrelationships have changed over time.   Children's literature, as selected for this bibliography, integrates multicultural men's and women's histories into "people's history."[6] While care was taken to exclude books that were sexist or racist in their viewpoint, the realism of sex roles and attitudes for a given time, place, and culture was carefully considered, and often noted in the section of the book citation titled "Content for Further Development."

Beyond the framework of time and location west of the Mississippi River and prior to 1900, several exceptional books have been included. The experiences of European immigrants are described with compassion and verity in *The Long Way to a New Land* by Joan Sandin.[7] This Swedish family's experience in crossing the Atlantic Ocean is typical of many European immigrants. Anne Pellowski's series of four books about Polish immigrant families in Wisconsin is included because their reasons for immigration, ethnic detail of family life, and the gradual assimilation of Anna's family are universal to many other immigrant families.[8]

Literary quality was an essential consideration. A good story that is well-told will ". . . carry the youngster along as a participant in the historical narrative."[9] While family life and children's lives are often the most motivating themes of children's literature, the setting and character development of the selected volumes convey authenticity and generate the interest of the prospective reader or listener. Both fiction and non-fiction books were selected as being supplementary to the content usually found in social studies textbooks, although the emphasis was placed on fictional works.

The non-fiction books included are of high interest, knowledgeable, but not encyclopedic in style. The 1988 Newbery Award winner, Russell Freedman, demonstrates these criteria of literary quality in his non-fiction books, *Children of the Wild West*, *Cowboys of the Wild West*, *Indian Chiefs*, and *Buffalo Hunt*.[10] Freedman's books are both informative and maintain the reader's interest throughout the narrative, with the assistance of authentic archival photographs. While preference in books will vary from one child to the next, this bibliography provides a range of setting, character, time frame, and writing styles allowing for such individual differences.

To aid in the selection of books, the information about each book is conveyed through standard bibliographic data and additional information as follows:

BOOK TITLE
AUTHOR
PUBLISHER, DATE OF PUBLICATION
ILLUSTRATOR
FICTION/NON-FICTION
INTERNATIONAL STANDARD BOOK NUMBER (ISBN)

READABILITY LEVEL
DESCRIPTORS
    Geographic Location
    Dates
    Main Characters (race, sex, age, nationality)

SYNOPSIS
ILLUSTRATIONS
STRENGTHS OF THE BOOK
CONTENT FOR FURTHER DEVELOPMENT

In each book citation, the Descriptors define the Geographic Location, Dates, and Main Characters, including their race, sex, age, and nationality. Through the Synopsis, an assessment of the Illustrations, the Strengths of the Book, and the Content for Further Development, the reader will be able to ascertain how best to select volumes for use with children.

Each of the books included in this bibliography was subjected to four standardized readability scales: The Fog Index of Printed Materials, the Flesch Scale of Readability, the Fry Readability Formula, and the Bormuth Readability Index Formula. To determine the readability level(s) of each book, we took text samples at random from each volume and applied the Readability Index Program by David Pinters, as used by the University of Michigan.[11]

As David Pinters explains in the software documentation, the Fog Index, as developed by Robert Gunning, is a formula based upon the average sentence length and the number of words with three syllables or more. The Bormuth Readability Index Formula, as provided by the University of Michigan, considers the variance between the number of letters and the number of words. The Flesch scale is based on a "Reading Ease" formula which includes the average sentence length (in words) and the number of syllables (in a 100-word sample). The Fry Readability Formula, developed by Edward Fry along with the Rutgers University Reading Center, is based on a graph plotting the average number of sentences per one hundred words versus the average number of syllables per one hundred words.

Reading specialists have varying opinions on the validity of these readability scales and undoubtedly they have their favorites. For this reason, these four scales were included to help teachers and librarians determine appropriate grade levels and reading audiences for particular books.

During the process of identifying and selecting the children's literature about *Peoples of the American West*, it became evident that homesteading and settling in the Great Plains from the Dakotas to Texas was the most popular topic chosen by the children's authors. The overland journeys and wagon trains west, books with Native Americans as the protagonists, immigration and the immigrant experiences were themes in large numbers of books. Surprisingly, girls and women were most often the central characters, regardless of setting or time frame. Considering the cultural impact of the Hispanic peoples, particularly in the Southwest, it was dismaying to find so few books about Hispanics. Black people in the West are represented in only a few books, as are Asians. In Chapter Two, "Analysis of Children's Historical Literature of the American West," the contents, viewpoints, and omissions of the literature will be further discussed.

In Chapter Three, "Learning Activities for Developing Historical Perspectives through Children's Literature," the learning experiences for children are grouped under four major concepts: time, place, change, and multicultural peoples. The range of learning activities will provide depth of experiences for independent readers and for groups of children from early elementary grades to middle school. While many of the activities are keyed to specific books in the bibliography, most activities may be applied to a wide range children's historical literature.

In no way will children's historical literature convey the whole story of any time or place in history. Through application of the criteria for selection, teachers, parents, and librarians will be able to add to this bibliography. As children are involved in the learning activities described in Chapter Three, they will expand their historical perspectives. Through the use of literature "beyond the basal" textbooks, along with the related learning experiences, the history of the American West will take on a new realism and multiculturalism for children and the adults who read with them.

∞∞∞∞∞∞∞∞∞∞∞

NOTES

1 Laura Ingalls Wilder, *Little House on the Prairie* (New York: Harper and Row, 1935), and other "Little House" books. Brett Harvey, *My Prairie Year: Based on the Diary of Elenore Plaisted* (New York: Holiday House, 1986); Waheenee, as told to Gilbert L. Wilson, *Waheenee: An Indian Girl's Story* (St. Paul, MN: Webb Publishing Co., 1927; reprint, Lincoln: University of Nebraska Press, 1981); Ruthanne Lum McCunn, *Pie-Biter* (San Francisco: Design Enterprises of San Francisco, 1983); Patricia MacLachlan, *Sarah, Plain and Tall* (New York: Harper and Row, 1985).

2 "The Best of the West," *The MAILBOX, The Idea Magazine for Teachers, Intermediate Edition* 8 (May/June 1986) : 19.

3   Advertisement for *Macmillan Instant Activities Program,* entitled "Now Make Your Classroom a Showplace of Creative Teaching!" in *Instructor* 98 (September 1988) : [75]

4   For a specific description of reading "beyond the basal" readers, including book lists, see California State Department of Education, *Recommended Readings in Literature, Kindergarten through Grade Eight* (Sacramento, CA: State Department of Education, 1986). See also, Marcella Gruber and Catherine Surdovel, "Using Children's Literature Across the Curriculum," *Learning 86* 15 (September 1986) : 56-57.

5   For additional nonsexist and nonracist criteria, see the following filmstrips produced by the Council on Interracial Books for Children, *Identifying Sexism and Racism in Children's Books,* Parts 1 and 2 (1978); *Unlearning Asian American Stereotypes* (1981); *Unlearning Chicano and Puerto Rican Stereotypes* (1982); and *Unlearning Indian Stereotypes* (1978).

6   Mary Kay Thompson Tetreault, "Rethinking Women, Gender, and the Social Studies," *Social Education* 51 (March 1987) : 178.

7   Joan Sandin, *The Long Way to a New Land* (New York: Harper and Row, 1981).

8   Anne Pellowski, *First Farm in the Valley: Anna's Story* (New York: Philomel Books, 1982); *Winding Valley Farm: Annie's Story* (New York: Philomel, 1982); *Stairstep Farm: Anna Rose's Story* (New York: Philomel, 1981); and *Willow Wind Farm: Betsy's Story* (New York: Philomel, 1981).

9 Raymond Allen, "Jamie and Kit Collier: The Writer and the Historian," *Teaching Pre K-8* 18 (January 1988) : 36.

10 Russell Freedman, *Children of the Wild West* (Boston: Houghton Mifflin, 1983); *Cowboys of the Wild West* (Boston: Houghton Mifflin, 1985); *Indian Chiefs* (New York: Holiday House, 1987); and *Buffalo Hunt* (New York: Holiday House, 1988).

11 Readability Index Program Rel [198?], Delta Software Company, [Ann Arbor, MI]

Chapter Two

Analysis of Children's Historical Literature of the American West

The search for appropriate historical literature for this bibliography began with a survey of the evaluative, published bibliographies of children's literature and other reviews of children's books in print.[1] Numerous books that did not support the criteria for selection were discarded. The relative absence of Hispanic people, black people, and cultures other than white Americans was identified as the major omission. Settings in the mountain areas were scarce, except as part of the westward journey to the West Coast. However, through the process of evaluating children's literature based on the criteria of realism, literary quality, and availability, children's books rich in variety and authenticity of characters and settings were identified.

The settlement of the Great Plains from North Dakota to Texas by farm families was the most prominent theme of the literature. This theme brings to the fore children as protagonists and as responsible family members in the environment of the frontier and the early settlements. The overland journey, another important theme in the literature, also portrays children as contributing members of the family and of the wagon train. The theme of immigration and the immigrant experience substantiates the diversity of the peoples of the American West. Books with Native Americans as the protagonists represent another major multicultural theme. With children and their historically authentic families as central characters in historical events, present-day children will understand those events through another child's experiences.

The decision to exclude folktales and myths omits, for example, the raucous good humor of the Pecos Bill stories and the beauty of Paul Goble's tales and illustrations.[2] Children, essentially concrete in their thinking, will more readily apply and integrate realistic literature than myths and folklore into their developing historical perspectives. As manifestations of cultures and religious beliefs, myths and folklore tend to teach " . . . what's behind literature and the arts, it teaches you about your own life."[3] The inner meanings and mysticism of folktales and myths demonstrate the universality of some themes and the infinite variations and inventiveness of the story tellers throughout time and across cultures. The wit and humor of oral tradition found in folktales will appeal to children.[4] Myths and folklore are appropriate literary and cultural corollaries for developing historical perspective. However, children who may have difficulty differentiating among the "olden days" of King Arthur, Red Cloud or their classroom teacher's childhood, will need assistance in appreciating the anthropological knowledge and analysis inherent in myth and folktales.

Gender and Characters. One expected problem in the literature search was that there would be insufficient numbers of books in which girls and women were the central characters. Instead, females as the main protagonists outnumbered boys and men, two to one. A possible explanation may be that the authors, predominantly women in this genre, write for their traditionally identified readers--elementary school girls. As the boys in the elementary grades are made aware of the exciting adventures of the appealing, authentic people in historical literature for children, we may hope to see more young male readers.

Concern for integrating women's history into the elementary curriculum will be well served by the books selected for this bibliography. Children's historical fiction, because of its emphasis on children's lives and family life, often illustrates the integration of women's history and multicultural histories into "people's history."[5] Historical fiction provides the setting in which the lives of women, girls, men, and boys reflect the appropriate sex roles for a given time, place, and culture. While historically appropriate sex roles may imply sexism when interpreted in our contemporary setting, the sex roles illustrate the historical perspective of changing interrelationships and responsibilities. The literature portrays both female and male characters in traditional roles and settings, and in adventurous, non-traditional situations. Children need to know that the ordinary people, much like themselves and their families, were the real people of the American West who carried their traditions to the settings where new ways of life evolved.

The adventures of girls most often seem to be relatively conventional, real-life experiences as in *The Snowbird* by Patricia Calvert.[6] Orphaned, teenaged Willanna and her six-year-old brother travel to the Dakota Territory to live with their aunt and uncle. Her adventure is that of growing up without her parents and coming to grips with her destiny. In *Meet Kirsten: An American Girl* and *Kirsten Learns a Lesson: A School Story* by Janet Beeler Shaw, a Swedish immigrant girl en route to Minnesota faces the death of her best friend. After the family gets settled, Kirsten attends school, learns to speak English, and makes new friends. Many of Kirsten's problems are those of any child who has moved to a new community. Seven-year-old Faith, the central character in *The Josefina Story Quilt* by Eleanor Coerr, pursues an appropriate girl's task of the 1850s as she pieces her quilt while the family travels west.

For both white settlers and Native Americans, the settlement of white people in the American West was a period of transition. The family stories of white people and of Native Americans tell of the roles that women and girls pursued in preserving their cultures through establishing and maintaining their family homes during this period of change. The girls and women of the Ingalls family in the "Little House" series and the Pellowski family in *First Farm in the Valley* and its sequels fulfill the nurturing, traditional, but changing roles of white females in rural families on the frontier and in the early-day settlements.[7] The autobiographical stories of family life of Native American women, such as *Waheenee: An Indian Girl's Story, Pretty Shield: Medicine Woman of the Crows*, and Zitkala-Sa's *American Indian Stories*, also portray traditional roles for girls and women in a period of displacement and change.[8]

The men and boys in these family stories fulfill their traditional roles as the providers and protectors of the family.

The appeal of these conventionally-portrayed people in this transitional period lies in their characterization as responsible members of strong, loving families who faced the joys and hardships of life as supportive units of interrelated people. The authenticity of these families and their adventures, as portrayed in the literature selected for *Peoples of the American West,* make them part of the heritage of the West, rather than merely a singular adventure to be briefly relished.

The girls and women within the setting of the frontier and early settlement days fulfilled their societies' conventional expectations and, as opportunities and needs arose, went beyond those expectations.   Being traditional in sex roles does not diminish the strength portrayed by the feminine characters in this bibliography. *Sarah, Plain and Tall* by Patricia MacLachlan portrays a woman strong in character and in dedication to caring for the family. As with many other women in the West in the late 1800s, Sarah, a mail-order bride, could fix the roof, drive the wagon, tend her garden, and love her new family. In *Words by Heart* by Ouida Sebestyen, eleven-year-old Lena, an obedient daughter, copes with rejection by members of the white community and with the death of her non-violent father. Lena's courage, strength of character, religious faith, and belief in her father's dedication to non-violence are tested by the prejudice exhibited by whites against her black family. Although Lena is still a child, she is a moral, ethical heroine to be valued by children.

Schoolteacher Belle Warren takes over her dead fiancé's land claim with the help of thirteen-year-old Maud McPherson in *The Sodbuster Venture* by Charlene Joy Talbot. Belle and Maud are traditional in their concerns about caring for other people, educating the children, and establishing a school.[9] They are examples of how ordinary young women in the transitional setting of the frontier carried out extraordinary tasks such as developing and maintaining their homestead and surviving the devastation of the grasshopper attacks. They typify the Turner thesis that the settlers were part of "a form of society. . . whose social conditions result[ed] from the application of older institutions and ideas to the transforming influences of free land."[10]

In *Eight Mules from Monterey* by Patricia Beatty, librarian Lettie Ashmore and her two children journey into the mountains of California in 1916 with a wagon-load of books. In this story based on the journals of an actual librarian, the Ashmores meet many different people who are eager to have access to library outposts. The role of librarian in the early twentieth century is a conventional, sedate profession for a woman. This story of an adventurous librarian and her children driving eight mules through the mountains in order to deliver books, attests to the service role of America's public librarians. Lettie is another example of a western woman who is traditional in her nurturing role as a parent and her dedication to her service-oriented profession. At the same time, Lettie is non-traditional in the ways in which she combines home and work responsibilities by responding to the unique opportunities and needs of others created by the time and the setting.

A tale of early California, *Carlota* by Scott O'Dell, portrays a non-traditional Spanish girl, an accomplished rider and horse manager, who accompanies her father to a battle against the Americans in California. After the battle, Carlota compassionately nurses her father and an American soldier back to health.

Aunt Columbia, a feminist and social reformer, in *Hail Columbia* by Patricia Beatty, tackles the problems of women's suffrage, the human rights of minorities, temperance, and political corruption. Beatty's approach is humorous, but also delineates the motivations of this quintessential, but fictional social reformer.[11] In Margaret Crary's biography written for later elementary and middle school readers, *Susette La Flesche: Voice of the Omaha Indians*, the life of an American Indian social reformer is sympathetically depicted. Susette, sister of Francis La Flesche who wrote *The Middle Five: Indian Schoolboys of the Omaha Tribe*, was also educated by white people. She taught school on the reservation for a while, and then became a dedicated activist for Indian land and voting rights. She was a notable heroine who dedicated her life to helping her people.

The adventures of the central male characters are varied in their themes and often filled with excitement and danger. In *Buffalo Moon* by G. Clifton Wisler and *Moccasin Trail* by Eloise Jarvis McGraw, the boys who are the protagonists run away from their homes and then come into contact with Indians. The run-away theme is believable for boys of the nineteenth century as is the broader theme of the rites of passage, including loyalty to friends and self-sufficiency. In the true story based on the diaries of Moses Schallenberger, *To California By Covered Wagon* by George R. Stewart, a seventeen-year-old Swiss immigrant spends the winter alone in a cabin in the mountains. In *An Orphan for Nebraska* by Charlene Joy Talbot, orphaned Kevin O'Rourke, an eleven-year-old Irish immigrant, survives the streets of New York on his own for a while. Then, through the help of the Children's Aid Society, he is sent west with other children to be adopted by families in Nebraska. Lynne Gessner's *Navajo Slave* tells of Straight Arrow, an eleven-year-old Navajo boy who is captured by Ute Indians, then sold as a slave to the Spanish. As a slave, he works with horses, befriends his owner's son, and plots his escape. In *The Middle Five: Indian Schoolboys of the Omaha Tribe,* Francis La Flesche gives an autobiographical account of his mission school education. The friendship among the boys at the boarding school is filled with humorous, boyish pranks and loyalty while they try to overcome their homesickness and subvert the efforts of the missionaries to make them into "make-believe white men."[12]

In several books, the fathers die or are incapacitated, leaving adolescent boys to take on the traditional responsibility of caring for the family. In *The Thundering Prairie* by Mary A. Hancock, fourteen-year-old Benjy participates in the land run to the Cherokee Strip after both his father and his older brother are injured. Fifteen-year-old Fritz, a German immigrant, becomes the head of the family when his father dies in *The Obstinate Land* by Harold Keith. A variation of this theme is found in *Frontier Farmer: Kansas Adventures* by Catherine E. Chambers. Thirteen-year-old Matt Foster and his mother decide to stay in Kansas after his father dies. William Lee, a former slave, and his thirteen-year-old son are hired to help run the farm. In the conflicts between ranchers and farmers, the Foster farm is damaged by the "nightriders." The Fosters and the Lees catch those responsible and then convince the townspeople not to hang the criminals.

Facing the Enemy by Dean Hughes and *Squaw Man's Son* by Evelyn Sibley Lampman depict teenaged boys and their families caught in the frightening web of intolerance. Joseph Williams and his brother in *Facing the Enemy* keep their Mormon family together after their father is killed. As they try to find a community where they can live peacefully, the brothers have to face violence and persecution of the Mormons by the other settlers.[13] The distasteful title, *Squaw Man's Son,* conveys the prejudice and alienation faced by thirteen-year-old Billy Morrison, the son of a white father and a Modoc Indian mother. The relocation battle between the Modocs and United States Army along the border of Oregon and California in 1873 is based on fact, while the Morrisons are fictitious, but believable characters.

In another group of books, boys and girls, usually siblings, survive hardships and dangers by working together. Honoré Morrow's *Seven Alone* and *For Ma and Pa: On the Oregon Trail, 1844* by Wilma Pitchford Hays tell the story based in fact of the survival of the Sager children who continue the trek to Oregon after their parents die along the way. While thirteen-year-old John Sager is the leader, it is the cooperation and family unity among the seven children that contribute to their successful journey of seven hundred miles on foot. In *Save Queen of Sheba* by Louise Moeri, a twelve-year-old white boy, King David, and his six-year-old sister, Queen of Sheba, survive an Indian attack on their wagon train. Through their own resourcefulness, they find their way along the trail and rejoin the other survivors. In Catherine E. Chambers' realistic account of the journey west, *Wagons West: Off to Oregon,* Jason, the elder brother, goes home to Virginia after the death of his parents to bring his younger brother and sister to his home in Oregon. The tale of the journey west by wagon train is filled with factual information, such as how much flour, salt, and dried beans were purchased for the journey, and how each person, including the children, had their responsibilities. In *A Family Apart* by Joan Lowery Nixon, a destitute widow in New York decides to send her children on the orphan train operated by the Children's Aid Society so that they can have a chance for a better life. Frances Mary, the oldest daughter, disguises herself as a boy so that she will have a better chance of staying with her little brother in order to care for him.

The portrayals of siblings within the more commonplace family events are found in a few volumes based on reminiscences of prairie settlers. *The Price of Free Land* is based on the homesteading recollections of Treva Adams Strait. Within the setting of the three-year homestead residency requirement, Strait describes the everyday events, such as washing clothes, going to school, and the daily chores. Photographs of the family and their home add to the realism of this pioneer account of Nebraska in 1914 to 1916. In *My Prairie Year: Based on the Diary of Elenore Plaisted*, Brett Harvey edited his grandmother's diary. Children's responsibilities are described as essential to the well-being of the homesteading family. The non-fiction book, *The Story of the Homestead Act* by R. Conrad Stein, will supply the historical background information about homesteading and everyday family life.

The Immigrants. Among the settlers of the American West featured in the children's literature are the immigrants. Children will have a difficult time knowing that people other than white American citizens followed the trails and made their homes in the West. A few books give accounts of the trip across the Atlantic by European immigrants. Swedish immigrant families are the central characters in Joan Sandin's *The Long Way to a New Land*, and Janet Beeler Shaw's *Meet Kirsten: An American Girl*. The true story of her Mormon family's journey from Switzerland to Utah is told by Mary Ann Hafen in *Recollections of a Handcart Pioneer of 1860: A Woman's Life on the Mormon Frontier*. The emotions of the European immigrants as well as the settings are beautifully and accurately illustrated by Diane Goode in *Watch the Stars Come Out* by Riki Levinson. The rich combination of text and illustrations convey the immigration experience for early elementary children.

The Norwegian Isaacsen family traveled from Omaha to the Dakota Territory for land in *Frontier Dream: Life on the Great Plains* by Catherine E. Chambers. Linda Lehmann's two-book sequence, *Better than a Princess* and *Tilli's New World*, describe many of the problems facing Tilli's German family, such as earning a living, the language barriers, and maintaining their heritage. Beginning with *First Farm in the Valley: Anna's Story*, Anne Pellowski chronicles four generations of her Polish family through *Winding Valley Farm, Stairstep Farm,* and *Willow Wind Farm.* Through the author's careful attention to ethnic detail and setting, the immigrant experience is told with good humor and enduring family values. Through the sequence of the four generations, the acculturation of the family is seen, as well as their pride in their heritage.

The West Coast is the setting for several books about Asian immigrants. While the stories are interesting, children need to know more about the conditions of the Asian Exclusion Act which kept Asian families from immigrating. Male Chinese railroad workers are the central characters in *Pie-Biter* by Ruthanne Lum McCunn and Kathleen Chang's *The Iron Moonhunter.* Kay Haugaard's *China Boy* seeks his fortune in the gold fields of California. In *Samurai of Gold Hill* by Yoshiko Uchida, Koichi and his father immigrate from Japan to California. Their attempts to establish a silkworm farm fail, but the strength and ethnicity of the characters and their values as they meet with prejudice and hardship make this an exceptional book about the immigrant experience. While this story takes place in 1869, there are many parallels with the experiences of more recent Asian immigrants. Laurence Yep's *Dragonwings,* another story of a father and son, is told through the experience of Moon Shadow, a Chinese boy who comes to California in 1903 to live with his father, a member of the Company of the Peach Orchard Vow, a Chinese laundry in Chinatown. The members of the Company live as an extended family, surviving the devastation of the San Francisco earthquake, and supporting one another in this period of blatant prejudice against Asian immigrants. The immigrant dream of success in the new world through hard work and sacrifice comes within reach as Moon Shadow's father, Windrider, seeks to build a biplane of his own design.

Ethnic Representation. The strength of the immigrant stories included in *Peoples of the American West* lies in the ability of the authors to maintain the ethnicity of the characters in their new environments. The characters are not dependent upon becoming "Americans" for acceptance, but are valuable, competent human beings because of their intelligence, resourcefulness, and their abilities. The out-dated "melting pot" view of the Americanization of immigrants is replaced in the books cited by respect for the diverse heritages of the multi-cultural peoples who are the citizens of the American West.

However, few ethnic or cultural groups other than Native Americans are included in the children's historical literature of the American West. Identification with national origins and ethnicity is scarce at this point in children's literature, but seems to be gaining recognition in communities where ethnic heritages are celebrated through Oktoberfests, Hispanic Festivals, Norwegian Days, Bavarian Festivals, Czech Days, and other ethnic events. The scarcity in the literature of the immigrants' cultural manifestations may be due in part to the mission of American public education of the late nineteenth and early twentieth centuries of Americanizing the immigrants. Recognition of the diversity among Americans is hampered by children's ignorance of personal, state, and national history. Reading these exemplary stories of immigration will encourage children, their parents, librarians and teachers to seek further knowledge about the origins of their families and of others.

Stories about the black people of the American West are even more scarce than those about Asians. Black people are the central characters in only four books included in this bibliography: *Wagon Wheels* by Barbara Brenner; *Frontier Farmer: Kansas Adventure* by Catherine E. Chambers; *Words by Heart* by Ouida Sebestyen; and *Walk the World's Rim* by Betty Baker.[14] The opportunities for homesteading and owning land for the black farmers of *Wagon Wheels* and *Frontier Farmer* contrast with the devastating experiences of the sharecroppers in *Words by Heart*. Esteban, the black slave in *Walk the World's Rim*, is a strong role model for the Indian Chief's son and for present-day readers. In *Wagon Wheels*, based on a true story, eleven-year-old Johnny Muldie and his two younger brothers are self-sufficient and responsible for each other when left on their own in the small community of Nicodemus, Kansas, for four months while their father searches for better land. They then follow their father's map for 150 miles to their new land claim. In these books, the well-developed characters are admirable people whose diverse roles are in keeping with the times and events of the stories. The appeal of these strong characters and the settings of their stories lies in the realism of their humanity and their adventures.

The most puzzling cultural omission is that of the underrepresented Hispanics. Betty Baker's *Walk the World's Rim* and *A Stranger and Afraid*, set in the American Southwest in the 1540s, have as the main characters male Indians, Spaniards, and the black slave, Esteban. The other books with Hispanic characters included in this bibliography are set in California, between 1818 and the 1850s. Patricia Beatty's *The Bad Bell of San Salvador*, Eleanor Coerr's *The Bell Ringer and the Pirates*, and Scott O'Dell's *Carlota*, include some aspects of Mexican and Spanish family life. These books are undoubtedly worth reading, but they cannot account for the tremendous Mexican and Spanish impact on the culture of the Southwest. In children's historical literature, there remain large voids in portraying the rich influence Hispanic cultures between the time of Spanish conquistadors, the missions of California, and the late twentieth century.

Present-day children of Hispanic heritages need to have their ancestors portrayed as appealing individuals and families with the warmth and the ethnic authenticity found in the Pellowski series and in the Laura Ingalls Wilder books. The spring 1989 publication of *Spanish Pioneers of the Southwest* by Joan Anderson with photographs by George Ancona, may be the beginning of a welcomed trend to recognize the Hispanic heritage through this account of a Spanish family who made their home in what is now New Mexico.[15]

Native Americans. Another major theme of the children's historical literature is found in books with Native Americans as the central characters. About one fourth of these books are autobiographical and written from the historical perspective of the Native American authors, including Pretty Shield as told to Frank Linderman, E-Yeh-Shure' (Blue Corn), Zitkala Sa (Gertrude Bonnin), Francis La Flesche, and Waheenee as told to Gilbert Wilson. While these books were not originally written for children, much of the content would be appropriate to read aloud, or to read with children. The customs and traditions of the cultures are described through accounts of family structure, responsibilities, and values. In the life stories of the Native

American authors, the transitions and conflicts between the Indian cultures and the white people's ways are conveyed poignantly through the authors' statements about their loss of their way of life and of their home environment. In the final chapter of *Waheenee: An Indian Girl's Story*, Waheenee describes her memories of the old days as ". . . but an old woman's dream. . . . Our Indian life, I know, is gone forever."[16]

The heart-breaking experiences of being forced to leave home and attend boarding schools operated by white people are told by Zitkala-Sa in *American Indian Stories*, Frank B. Linderman in *Pretty Shield: Medicine Woman of the Crows*, and Francis La Flesche in *The Middle Five: Indian Schoolboys of the Omaha Tribe*. While the goal of being educated and able to speak and write English was partially accepted by these authors, the method of forcibly removing children from their families, forbidding them to speak their own languages and maintain their customs was a dehumanizing destruction of the human spirit. However, each of these authors writes about their lives and families with affection, again demonstrating that basic human needs and integrity are universals that cut across cultural boundaries.

Based on documented true events, *Little Yellow Fur* by Wilma Pitchford Hays and Barbara Brenner's *Wagon Wheels* tell of families and their positive contacts with Indians. In *Wagon Wheels*, Osage Indians bring food and fuel to the settlement at Nicodemus, Kansas, so that the black settlers can survive the harsh winter. *Little Yellow Fur* is based on the author's childhood in South Dakota in 1913. Six-year-old Susanna, nicknamed "Little Yellow Fur" by the Sioux Indians of the Rosebud Indian Reservation, helps her mother and the Sioux see each other simply as people who have many commonalities.

Everyday life in New Mexico, circa 1930, is portrayed in *I Am a Pueblo Indian Girl* by E-Yeh-Shure' and *In My Mother's House* written by Ann Nolan Clark, a long-term teacher of American Indians. These books are included because they are appropriate for young children by capturing traditional Indian life from the viewpoint of Indian children.

Conflict of Cultures. In other children's books, the central characters portray the interactions between the Native

Americans and other people. In Eleanor Coerr's *The Bell Ringer and the Pirates,* eight-year-old Pio, an Ahachmai Indian boy, is the hero of San Juan Capistrano Mission in the early 1800s when he warns his family and friends of the pirates' attack. The protagonists in *Buffalo Moon* by G. Clifton Wisler are adolescent boys, one white and one Comanche. In this story set in pre-Civil War Texas, the white boy is accepted by the Indians after he successfully completes their rites of passage. By contrast, Yvette Dumelle, the thirteen-year-old Chinook-French girl in *The Halo Wind* by Judith St. George, resists attempts by a well-meaning white family to take her to the mission school in Oregon. Through the characters of an adolescent boy and the great Cherokee Chief Sequoyah, this conflict of cultures is strongly portrayed in *Edge of Two Worlds* by Wyman Jones.

Russell Freedman's well-illustrated *Indian Chiefs* documents the lives of six great Indians leaders, Red Cloud, Satanata, Quanah Parker, Washakie, Joseph, and Sitting Bull, as they faced the problems of accepting the dictates of the United States government, or fighting for the land that was rightfully theirs. Freedman brings the historical accuracy needed for an assessment of the Indians wars, including the Battle of Wounded Knee Creek in 1890. Archival photographs, maps, and other illustrations make this book essential to understanding this period of conflict. *The Tipi: A Center of Native American Life* by David and Charlotte Yue, explains the structure of this dwelling place, its spiritual meaning, and role in the everyday life of the Great Plains Indians. The factual content and illustrations of these two books make them essential reading for an understanding of Native Americans.

Betty Baker's *A Stranger and Afraid* and *Walk the World's Rim,* cited earlier as books with Hispanic characters, have adolescent Indian boys as richly developed characters who come into contact with cultures vastly different from their own. Fourteen-year-old Chakoh, the Chief's son in *Walk the World's Rim,* meets Spaniards and their black slave, Esteban. Wichita Indian brothers, Sopete and Zabe, are captives of the Cicuyen Indians in *A Stranger and Afraid.* Sopete and Kima, a Pawnee captive, maintain their desire for freedom and their own beliefs. Sopete becomes concerned that his little brother is forgetting how to live as a Wichita as the eight-year-old Zabe becomes accustomed to the Cicuyen way of life. This theme of adapting to the captors' way of life shows up in other stories of captivity, such as *Wait for Me, Watch for Me, Eula Bee* by Patricia Beatty and *White Captives* by Evelyn Sibley Lampman. In these books, the latter based on fact, the white people's goal was to reclaim the white girls who were becoming at home with the lifestyles of their Indian captors.

In Scott O'Dell's *Sing Down the Moon* and Lampman's *White Captives*, strong female characters are held as captives. O'Dell tells this moving story from the Indian viewpoint of Bright Morning and two of her friends who escape from Spanish slavers only to be forced by United States soldiers to relocate to land three hundred miles from their home. The true story of Olive and Mary Ann Oatman is told sympathetically in *White Captives*, portraying both the hardships of captivity and the family structure of the Mohave Indians. The author's postscript briefly notes Olive's life after she is taken back to live with white people. Her lectures and writing about her experiences grew more negative as the years went by, and as other white people reacted to her accounts of enslavement.

Through these accounts of captivity, it is important to examine the custom of capturing enemies who became slaves in the context of warfare and as symbols of bravery among American Indians. This practice has some similarities to, but is a different situation from, capturing people for the purpose of enslavement and profit from the sale of slaves. The latter practice was pursued by some Native Americans and by some Spaniards. Through a narrow interpretation of captivity stories, children could easily come to the conclusion that all Indians and Spaniards enslaved people for profit. Rather than highlighting the sensationalism of captivity stories, each of the authors included in this bibliography has emphasized the inner strength of the central characters, their persistent human spirit, and their relationships with other captives and their captors.

It is appropriate that Native Americans figure prominently in the literature as protagonists and in relationship to other cultures. Their traditional lifestyles and ancestral lands are the settings of the journeys and settlements by other peoples. Care must be taken that the readers, with the help of their parents, teachers, and librarians, identify the specific tribe of American

Indians of a given time and place and differentiate between the past and the present. Much of the stereotyping of American Indians comes from the assumption that all Indians are the same, regardless of tribes, time, or place.

In this context of insufficient information, children may learn stereotypes through reinforcing their assumptions. For example, the September 1988, issue of a popular, well-regarded periodical for elementary teachers has a beautiful poster of George Catlin's portrait of Strutting Pigeon, wife of White Cloud, and their daughter.[17] In the accompanying article, a number of learning activities are recommended, including asking children to pretend that they are living in an Indian village, pretend to be members of an unidentified Indian tribe, and to make paper representations of Indian clothing from an unknown tribe and time frame. Children's responses to such "learning activities" will be based on their limited knowledge and experiences. The article provides no information about the identity, tribe, time frame, or location of White Cloud, his wife, and daughter. The real people and events become invisible in this approach which denigrates Native Americans in general, and White Cloud and his family specifically. A few minutes with a reference book would reveal that Waubeshiek, or White Cloud, 1794-1841, was a prophet and advisor to the Sac Chief Black Hawk during the Black Hawk War against the white settlers and United States soldiers, 1832-1833, in Illinois and Wisconsin. During the battle of Bad Axe River, Black Hawk's request to surrender was ignored, while most of his band, including women and children, were killed. White Cloud had prophesized victory for Black Hawk and was imprisoned with Black Hawk and other survivors. The real people and real events tell a dramatic story of the courageous people who tried to preserve their land and their way of life.[18]

The myths and legends of the Native Americans have often been used with children as substitutes for learning about real people and real events. The myths and legends of any culture will enrich children's understandings of that culture to the degree to which children can differentiate between reality and fantasy, and identify the likenesses among cultures. For example, "The Ghost Horse Cycle" by Jamake Highwater will provide to the informed adolescent or adult reader, rich insights about the beliefs and changes in the lives of Northern Plains Indians over the course of three generations.[19] Highwater's mystical, poetic, allegorical style will be difficult for younger readers who may have little or no accurate information about the various Indian cultures and may interpret these books simply as fantasy. When children have an informational base drawn from history, anthropology, and realistic historical literature, they will begin to understand the complexities of the Native American myths and the myths of other cultures without losing sight of the real people who told these stories and lived by the values expressed through the myths and legends.[20]

Throughout the children's historical literature of the American West, there are commonplace children and families as representative, multicultural, authentic peoples. Some of their stories are based in fact, while others are fictional tales with realistic settings. As a genre, the children's books do justice to the life and times of many but not all of the peoples of the American West. The major themes of the journeys to America, the overland trips to the West, and settling in the West, depict the diverse heritages of white and black Americans and of European and Asian immigrants.

When first considering children's literature of the American West, the American classics of Laura Ingalls Wilder come to mind. Through this bibliography, readers will find additional authors to enrich and expand their historical perspectives while enjoying the well-told tales. For early elementary readers, Wilma Pitchford Hays and Eleanor Coerr are especially notable through their stories included in this bibliography of the westward journey, settling in the West, and life in a West Coast mission. Patricia Beatty's good-humored tales and memorable characters will be enjoyed by independent readers in later elementary and middle school, and as read-aloud books.[21] The non-fiction books by Russell Freedman and R. Conrad Stein blend archival documents, photographs and historical information to provide the historical context for the children's historical literature. Brett Harvey has used archival sources such as his grandmother's diary as the basis for his books in which children from another time tell their own stories.

While the children's literature is interesting in and of itself, the broader context of the historical and social settings must also be explored through the non-fiction books included in this bibliography, the social studies textbooks, and other references. The goal of helping children develop their historical perspectives of the American West will be best served through actively involving the children in the learning activities described in Chapter Three. The multicultural peoples of the American West will come alive for children through this combination of literature, social studies, and learning activities.

∞∞∞∞∞∞∞∞∞∞∞∞∞

NOTES

1 See "References", p. 215-222.

2 Pecos Bill stories will be found in Anne Malcolmson, *Yankee Doodle's Cousins* (Boston: Houghton Mifflin Company, 1941; reprint, Boston: Houghton Mifflin, 1969); and the more recent Steven Kellogg, *Pecos Bill: A Tall Tale* (New York: Morrow, 1986). Two favorites from Paul Goble are *The Gift of the Sacred Dog* (Scarsdale, NY: Bradbury, 1980), and *The Girl Who Loved Wild Horses* (Scarsdale, NY: Bradbury, 1978).

3 Joseph Campbell with Bill Moyers, *The Power of Myth* (New York: Doubleday, 1988), 11.

4 For folktales from a specific state, contact the State Library of that state, and the state university press. For example, the University Press of New Mexico, Albuquerque, offers ten folklore and myth titles in their Fall 1988 catalog, including the reprint of Tony Hillerman's *The Boy Who Made Dragonfly: A Zuni Myth* (New York: Harper and Row, 1972).

5 Mary Kay Thompson Tetreault, "Rethinking Women, Gender, and the Social Studies," *Social Education*   51 (March 1987) : 177-178.

6 All children's books and authors in the remainder of this chapter, not otherwise documented, are included in the annotated, selected Bibliography.

7 Kathryn Adam, "Laura, Ma, Mary, Carrie, and Grace: Western Women as Portrayed by Laura Ingalls Wilder," in Susan Armitage and Elizabeth Jameson, editors, *The Women's West* (Norman: University of Oklahoma Press, 1987), 95-110.

8 For recent assessments of western women's history, the following are recommended for the adult reader: Susan Armitage and Elizabeth Jameson, editors, *The Women's West* (Norman: University of Oklahoma Press, 1987);   Joanna L. Stratton, *Pioneer Women: Voices from the Kansas Frontier* (New York: Simon and Schuster, 1981);   Lillian Schlissel, *Women's Diaries of the Westward Journey* (New York: Schocken Books, 1982); and Gretchen M. Bataille and Kathleen Mullen Sands, *American Indian Women: Telling Their Lives* (Lincoln: University of Nebraska Press, 1984).   In *Prairie Women: Images in American and Canadian Fiction* (New Haven: Yale University Press, 1986), Carol Fairbanks interprets the literature written by prairie women authors and their portrayals of the land and the people.

9 For further information about schoolwomen in the West, see Mary Hurlbut Cordier, "Prairie Schoolwomen, Mid-1850s to 1920s, in Iowa, Kansas, and Nebraska," *Great Plains Quarterly* 8 (Spring 1988) : 102-119.

10 Frederick Jackson Turner, "The Problem of the West," in Ray A. Billington, editor, *Frontier and Section: Selected Essays of Frederick Jackson Turner*   (Englewood Cliffs, NJ: Prentice-Hall, 1961), 63.

11 Glenda Riley explores the role of women as social reformers in Chapter 6, "Strong-Minded Women," in *Frontierswomen: The Iowa Experience* (Ames: Iowa State University Press, 1981), 136-170.

12 Francis La Flesche, *The Middle Five: Indian Schoolboys of the Omaha Tribe*   (Madison: University of Wisconsin, 1900, 1963; reprint, Lincoln: University of Nebraska, 1978), xx.

13 For additional books about the Mormon experiences in the West, contact the Deseret Book Company, P. O. 30178, Salt Lake City, Utah, 84130.

14 Reviews of books by Betty Baker not included in this Bibliography will be found in Lynda G. Adamson, *A Reference Guide to Historical Fiction for Children and Young Adults* (New York: Greenwood Press, 1987). Those books set in the American West by Betty Baker are: *And One Was a Wooden Indian*   (Macmillan, 1970), Apache Indians, 1860s;   *Do Not Annoy the Indians* (Macmillan, 1968), Arizona Territory, 1850s; *The Dunderhead War*   (Harper and Row, 1967),   German immigrants, New Mexico, 1840s; and *Killer-of-Death* (Harper and Row, 1963), Apache Indians, 1850s.

15 Joan Anderson, photographs by George Ancona, *Spanish Pioneers of the Southwest,* (New York: E.P. Dutton, 1989).

16   Waheenee as told to Gilbert L. Wilson, *Waheenee: An Indian Girl's Story* (St. Paul, MN: Webb Publishing Company, 1927; reprint, Lincoln: University of Nebraska Press, 1981), 176.

17   Nancy Roucher, "Observe a quiet dignity," *Instructor* 98 (September 1988) : 58; and accompanying poster, "Strutting Pigeon, Wife of White Cloud by George Catlin," *Instructor* 98 (September 1988): [59-66].

18   *The New Columbia Encyclopedia,* 1975 ed., s.v. "Black Hawk War" and "Waubeshiek."

19   Jamake Highwater, *Legend Days* (New York: Harper and Row, 1984); *The Ceremony of Innocence* (New York: Harper and Row, 1985); and *I Wear the Morning Star* (New York: Harper and Row, 1986).

20   For an extensive listing of literature about and by American Indians, see   Gretchen M. Bataille, *American Indian Literature: A Selected Bibliography for Schools and Libraries* (Pomona, CA: National Association Interdisciplinary Ethnic Studies, Ethnic Studies Department, California State Polytechnic University, 1981).

21   Reviews of books by Patricia Beatty not included in this Bibliography will be found in Lynda G. Adamson, *A Reference Guide to Historical Fiction for Children and Young Adults* (New York: Greenwood Press, 1987). Those books set in the American West by Patricia Beatty are: *Blue Stars Watching* (Morrow, 1969), San Francisco, 1860s; *Bonanza Girl* (Morrow, 1962), Idaho Territory, 1880s; *How Many Miles to Sundown* (Morrow, 1974), American Southwest, 1880s; *Just Some Weeds From the Wilderness* (Morrow, 1978), Oregon, 1870s; *Lacy*

Makes a Match (Morrow, 1979), California, 1890s; *Me, California Perkins* (Morrow, 1968), California, 1880s; *The Nickel-Plated Beauty* (Morrow, 1964), Washington Territory, 1880s; *O The Red Rose Tree* (Morrow, 1972), Washington State, 1890s; *The Queen's Own Grove* (Morrow, 1966), California, 1880s; *Red Rock Over the River* (Morrow, 1973), Arizona Territory, 1880s; and *Something to Shout About* (Morrow, 1976), Idaho Territory, 1870s.

Chapter Three

Learning Activities
for Developing Historical Perspectives
Through Children's Literature

Through reading beyond the basal social studies textbook, children will begin to develop concepts about other times, places, and the people who lived the events. Book reports of a traditional format in which the title, author, main characters, and prominent events are stated may begin the process of concept development. For most children, the book report will not provide an internalization of these events which are beyond the experiences of children. In dealing with the history of the American West, the major concepts to consider are those of time, place, change, and multicultural peoples. Children's concepts about people, other time periods, and other places can begin formation through reading realistic historical literature and actively responding to the content of the literature. This will best be achieved with the help of their parents, teachers, and librarians.

In this section, learning activities will be grouped under major concepts, with suggested purposes, procedures, and outcomes. It will be the choice of the teacher, librarian, or other adult to determine whether to individualize the activity or implement the learning experience with groups of children. Many of the activities can be adapted for use with early or later elementary children, and can be applied to read-aloud books and to a wide variety of books read independently by children.

ESTABLISHING THE SETTING, CHARACTERS AND PLOT

TO BEGIN: The Story Map. As the foundation for the learning activities related to children's literature, select a significant event from a read-aloud book and develop a story map with the children in which the events and relationships among the characters are shown in sequence, pictorially and through words and phrases. As children become familiar with the process of story mapping, they can individually map stories that they are reading independently. The information on a story map may be displayed as a diagram, an outline, or in the shape of some component of the story such as a covered wagon. Story maps may also take the form of a flow-chart, or a mobile, with the action of the story or the main character as the central portion of the mobile.

The **story map** will visually establish the multiple causes of events, problems, and changes, the interrelationships of the characters, and how the conflicts or problems in the story are resolved.

Major Components of the Story Map:

CHARACTERS: names; ages; sex; descriptions of physical characteristics and personalities; interests; motivations.

SETTING: dates or years; descriptions of the time and the place using adjectives from the story, including weather, land forms and environments.

PROBLEM(S): description of the problem(s); who has the problem, why it can/not be solved; cause and effects.

HOW THE PROBLEM WAS SOLVED: who solved the problem; how they solved the problem; results of the solution.

To establish an understanding of the characters, the setting, and plot, start with a story map, or develop the story map as a book is being read. The concurrent step is to establish comprehension of the setting of the story based on the concepts of place and of time.

∞∞∞∞∞∞∞∞∞∞∞∞

DEVELOPING THE CONCEPT OF PLACE

Among the most prevalent themes of children's historical literature are the experiences of families on the westward journey and settling in the West. Therefore, the concepts of place begin with locating "the West" and identifying where the contemporary readers live. Although young children may have few map skills, they can begin to work with maps as a way to locate places where the book characters lived. The following learning activities will aid in developing the concepts of location or place.

TO BEGIN: The Outline Map. Place a large outline map of the United States or of North America on the bulletin board. The map can be easily drawn by projecting a transparency of an outline map with the overhead projector. A four by six foot outline map on paper will allow for various items to be drawn on the map or attached to the map. Place the outline map near the standard wall map of the same scale which will show the physical features of the land and present-day political boundaries. This will allow for quick references between the two maps, including comparisons of "then and there" and "now and here."

Home Location: Prominently mark your community and other known places on the outline map as the starting points; then identify the locations of the events from children's books in a variety of ways as follows:

Book Titles, Main Characters, Place Names: First, write the book title, author, and illustrator on a 3" by 5" card. This establishes the basic idea that books have names, are written by authors, and illustrated by artists. Other information may be written or drawn on the card to indicate the main characters, the date, the place or location of the story, or a description of an event from the story. Attach the card to the outline map in the appropriate location to indicate the setting of the book. Add place names to the outline map as children read about towns, rivers, regions, mountains, and other places.

Land Forms and Environments: Help children visualize the location of the events from the book(s) by placing pictures from magazines, postcards, and photographs around the borders of the outline map. Connect the pictures of the land forms such as plains and mountains, or environments such as forests, prairies, and deserts, to the appropriate location on the map by attaching a length of yarn between the picture and the place. In this way the *prairie* of Laura Ingalls Wilder's *Little House on the Prairie* or *My Prairie Year* by Brett Harvey are visual images photocopied from the illustrations of the books and from other pictorial sources. Include contemporary pictures and postcards of your community. Compare the current, or "now," pictures of your community with the photocopies of "then" pictures from the children's books and from archival photographs and other pictures in library or museum collections. In this way, place and time begin to come together and children will begin to differentiate between the time frames of "now and then" and the locations of "here and there."

Mapping Journeys: For books that have events in several locations, create a symbol for the book and place the symbol on the map at each location. Additional information such as dates may be included with the symbols as needed or desired. Another way to show a journey is to draw the route directly on the outline map and label the events with dates and details. On the outline map, draw the trips west as portrayed in children's books. For young children, the journey portrayed in *The Josefina Story Quilt* by Eleanor Coerr can be drawn on the map. For later elementary youngsters, Laurie Lawlor's *Addie Across the Prairie* tells about a family's 500-mile trip from Iowa to the Dakota Territory to homestead. The vivid imagery and character development of Kathryn Lasky's *Beyond the Divide* will provide middle school readers with an understanding of the long wagon train journey from St. Joseph, Missouri, to California in 1849.

Map a Contemporary Trip: Using different colors or different symbols, students can map a contemporary trip west following the routes of the major highways such as United States Interstate 80. Note how Interstate 80 follows the wagon trails along the Platte River across Nebraska. Other such relationships of "now and then" will also be discovered. Modern-day railroad and air routes will show additional ways to compare routes of the past and the present.

Immigration Routes: On the outline map of the United States or the world map, label the region or countries of origin of the main characters and show their journeys or immigration routes. In addition to European immigrants, be sure to include the immigrants to the West Coast from China, Japan, and other Asian countries, and the immigrants from Mexico, Latin America, and Canada. Janet Beeler Shaw's *Meet Kirsten: An American Girl*, *Tilli's New World* by Linda Lehmann, and Yoshiko Uchida's *Samurai of Gold Hill* are examples of the immigrant experience.

Family Origins: Label the countries representing the origins of the present-day children's families. Ask parents to supply this information along with the dates of immigration. Many families may not know this information, but may be able to supply information about where their family has lived within the United States. This also represents valid information to place on the map in order to show children that many people have families that originated in other regions and nations.

Native American Lands: Show locations on the outline map where the Native Americans lived in the past and where they live today. Be sure to name each group, for as Russell Freedman points out in *Indian Chiefs*: "These tribes were as different from one another as the different nations of Europe."[1] Do not use tipis to mark where the Indians lived unless that Indian nation actually lived in tipis. Show the traditional lands of the Native Americans and the relocation routes to the reservations as a way of showing that Native American territories of the past were extensive as compared to their holdings today.

Distance: To convey concepts about distances, help children use the map scale to show how far a wagon train traveled in a day, a week, or a month. Ellen Levine's *If You Traveled West in a Covered Wagon* will provide background information about the trip for young children. *Overland to California in 1859: A Guide for Wagon Train Travelers,* compiled and edited by Louis M. Bloch, Jr., is a collection of maps, illustrations, advertisements, and information actually used by the overland pioneers. A storehouse of valuable information, *Overland to California in 1859* will be indispensable for later elementary and middle school readers. Compare the distances obtained from the children's fiction and non-fiction books with a contemporary trip by car in a day, a week, or a month. Although these distances could be graphed, drawing them on the outline map plots out the comparative distances in the context of the known place names from the children's experiences and from their reading.

∞∞∞∞∞∞∞∞∞∞∞∞∞

DEVELOPING THE CONCEPT OF ANOTHER TIME

To help children differentiate among the "olden days" of various generations, commence with the children's lives of today. Just as the outline map begins with locating the children's community, the study of another time starts with the present day and the children's span of years.

TO BEGIN: The Time Line. Use a long roll of shelf paper for a time line that is plotted in ten-year intervals. Construction of a time line may be expedited by using computer software such as Timeliner.[2] Extend dates on the time line from the earliest year to be included from the events of the children's books to the present decade.

The Present Decade: Children's Names, Birth Dates, and Significant Events. In the present decade, list the children's names, birth years, and events of personal significance such as starting school, the birth of a sibling, moving to a new home, or learning a new skill. Other notable events may be be identified with families, neighborhoods, communities, states, regions, nation, and the world. This array of events can be simplified for young children or adapted so that there will be correlation with the books that are being read. For this section of the time line, the children will need sufficient vertical space to plot out the information about their childhood years.

The Previous Generation: Plot information about the previous generation. This may be as simple as delineating the birth years of the teacher, librarian, or parents, and a few personally significant events in their lives as parallels to the children's time line. The time line will now show two generations.

Grandparents' Generation: Grandparents of the children may be the third generation to be plotted on the time line. For the three generational time line, a span of approximately fifty years will be displayed. Help children identify the content of the time line that demonstrates that the people in each generation had childhoods, although their childhoods occurred at different times. The time line establishes a visual representation of the known experiences of people who are familiar to the children.

Another Time and Place: Main Characters and Events. Now the children can move to the experiences of another time and place through the use of the time line. It will quickly become apparent that grandparents, teachers, parents, and librarians did not live during the olden days of covered wagons. The separation of the past and the present is a visual representation on the time line.

Although some historical books are general in time frame, others are quite specific. On the time line, plot the childhood years and personally significant events in the lives of main characters from the books with specific time frames. For books that are more general in time scope, work with children to determine the probable dates from context clues. This inquiry task will become easier as children become more familiar with the people and events of another time and place. The context clues found in the historical fiction, will be identified through using the non-fiction books included in the bibliography, other references, and the social studies textbook. For this inquiry task, Mabel Harmer's *The True Book of Pioneers* and *Children of the Wild West* by Russell Freedman will be of special value.

Significant Dates, Past and Present: Add other dates and events to the time line that have some personal relationship to children's lives, such as when their community was first settled, when their school, library, or their home was built, or when their state joined the Union. Current events may also be added to the time line. The time line now shows where the children themselves and the people they know are placed in time, and when the book characters lived.

∞∞∞∞∞∞∞∞∞∞∞∞∞∞∞

DEVELOPING THE CONCEPT OF CHANGE

The concept of change will easily be seen by children as they consider their own growth, development, and experiences as shown on the **time line**. The pictures of the past and present that are connected to the **outline map** also establish the foundations of the concept of change. Because changes in people's lives come from a variety of causes, the concept of change begins with cause and effect relationships. The **story map** shows the relationships among characters, their problems and conflicts and how they were resolved.

CAUSE AND EFFECT RELATIONSHIPS

Conflicts Between Cultures. Prominent among the cause and effect relationships in the history of the American West are the conflicts between cultures. Through **story maps, time lines,** and other tangible representations of cause and effect relationships, children will observe that antagonism among people has multiple causes and no simple solutions. While books that are appealing to children most often include conflicts and problems to be solved as part of the plots, those dealing with human rights and the conflicts of cultures are a large part of the historical perspective of the American West.

Examples of cultural conflicts may be found in Betty Baker's novels, *A Stranger and Afraid* and *Walk the World's Rim,* where the conflicts are among various Indian tribes and with the Spanish. Through the character development and the historical settings, the readers will find that both the Native Americans and the Spaniards had multiple problems based in the conflicts between cultures. In *Little Yellow Fur* by Wilma Pitchford Hays, the conflict is between white people and Indians. Through the person of little Susanna, both the white people and the Indians recognize their mutual concerns. In order to see cultural conflict from the perspective of the Native Americans, books such as *Pretty Shield: Medicine Woman of the Crow, Waheenee: An Indian Girl's Story,* and Francis La Flesche's *The Middle Five: Indian Schoolboys of the Omaha Tribe* must be included in the consideration of cultural conflicts.

The cultural conflicts between Asian immigrants and the white people of the West Coast are portrayed with sensitivity and depth in Laurence Yep's *Dragonwings* and Yoshiko Uchida's *Samurai of Gold Hill.* The black family in *Words By Heart* by Ouida Sebestyen lives an exemplary, peaceful life although they experience the worst of violent prejudice at the hands of white people. *Hail Columbia* by Patricia Beatty deals with human rights for women and minorities as seen through a family's often humorous experiences with their Aunt Columbia, a suffragette in Astoria, Oregon, in 1893.

Relationships: The Web of Characters and Events. Character relationships, both simple and complex, may be illustrated for read-aloud books with groups of children through a circular web. With the children, make large names tags for the main book characters involved in a prominent event. Children will assume the role of the characters as they each receive a name tag. If there are many conflicts and interdependencies among the characters, have the children sit in a circle. Give the end of a large ball of yarn to one child, who, as the character designated on the name tag, will select another character and tell how they are interdependent, in conflict with one another, or other information about their relationships. The first child holds on to the end of the yarn as it is to passed to the second person. As each character is identified, the yarn is passed to that character and a web is formed showing the interrelationships. Visually and physically, the characters' lives and actions are tied or webbed together. To emphasize interrelationships, have one main character pull on the yarn while everyone else holds on. All the other characters should feel the tug on the yarn and know that they are connected. Have the main character drop the yarn. When the other characters tug on the yarn, a tangle of yarn will result to symbolize the problems that ensue when relationships are broken or changed abruptly and when conflicts are not resolved.

Relationships: Linear Sequence of Characters and Events. For a sequence of events flowing from one character to another, have the children form a line connected by the yarn as their character is named. While this activity is simpler to perform than the web, it shows sequence of events more than the relationships among the characters.

THE INFLUENCE OF TECHNOLOGIES ON CHANGE

In children's visions of the present, technology may be represented by space travel, computers, and video games. The impact of technological changes on travel, communications, work, and everyday life is part of the concepts of time and change in relationship to the people of a specific time and place. Information about inventions such as the cotton gin and the McCormick reaper are often included in elementary social studies textbooks. However, few children grasp how these technologies significantly influenced everyday life at the time of their invention.

TO BEGIN: Now and Then Chart. To put technological changes into the context of daily life, first focus on events that have current meaning in the children's lives, such as children's household chores, favorite possessions, games and toys, foods and food preparation, school buildings, supplies, and equipment. Construct a "now and then" chart starting with the children's experiences of "now." Then fill in the same information about "then" as drawn from the children's books. After establishing the comparison of children of "now and then" proceed to other comparisons as appropriate to the grade level of the children and the content of the books. Use headings and sources such as:

1. **Foods, Household Chores, and Appliances.** See *The Little House Cookbook* by Barbara M. Walker, *Nebraska Pioneer Cookbook* by Kay Graber, and Mabel Harmer's *The True Book of Pioneers*.

2. **Schools, Classrooms, Buildings, Books, Supplies and Equipment.** For information about school experiences of the past, see *Kirsten Learns a Lesson* by Janet Beeler Shaw, Russell Freedman's *Children of the Wild West*, *The Middle Five* by Francis La Flesche, *Elder Brother* by Evelyn Sibley Lampman, *Tilli's New World* by Linda Lehmann, and" Little House" books by Laura Ingalls Wilder.

3. **Communications and Transportation.** See *The Story of the Golden Spike* by R. Conrad Stein and *The True Book of Pioneers* by Mabel Harmer.

4. **Farming Practices and Equipment.** See *The Story of the Homestead Act* by R. Conrad Stein, Mabel Harmer's *The True Book of Pioneers*, and other books listed under "Homesteading and Settling in the West."

5. **Health and Medicine.** Many of the stories of the American West include episodes about illnesses and death from a variety of causes. For specific accounts of the role of doctors and healers, see Pam Conrad's *Prairie Songs*, *Seven Alone* by Honoré Morrow, *Cassie's Journey: Going West in the 1860s* by Brett Harvey and Frank B. Linderman's *Pretty Shield: Medicine Woman of the Crows*. Note that changes in medicine may be the most significant technology in terms of preserving and enhancing life.

Other headings may include **entertainment, goods and services, manufacturing** or may be suggested by the children's literature. Select the comparisons that are most appropriate to the books being read, and that emphasize the historical content. Information to be included under each heading may be drawn solely from the children's books or may be the basis for further investigations.

THE INFLUENCE OF ENVIRONMENT ON CHANGE

The term environment must first be defined as the surrounding physical conditions of a specific place, combined with the social and cultural conditions of that place. The **outline map, time line,** and **story maps** will serve as the foundations for this concept inasmuch as the information available in these sources describes the physical conditions of specific times and places along with the social and cultural situations of the people of that time and place.

Comparing the Influence of Environments, Past and Present: To further develop an understanding of the influence of environment on change, ask children to draw a picture map of their favorite room at home or their classroom and include as many details as possible. For example, show the furniture, toys, games, books, and pets that may be present in this favorite room. Suppose your class had to move to another location, but all that could be moved had to fit inside one school bus along with the children. What objects, materials, and supplies would you move from your classroom and from any other favorite room at school? Or, suppose the child's family was moving to a new location and the only possessions that could be moved had to fit inside the family car along with the members of the family? Maybe the family could also have a very small trailer. What things would the child move from that favorite room?

Decision-Making Based on the Environment: The decision-making involved in the choices children made in the previous activities leads into the consideration of the environment of the destination point for the class or for the family. For example, the physical conditions, including climate and land forms, will determine what kind of clothing will be useful. The social and cultural setting will influence what family or school resources will be present in the new environment. Relate these present-day contrived decisions to the decisions made by the book characters.

The **Chart of Environmental Influences** will aid in developing this concept. To consider the environmental factors of another time increases children's historical perspectives. The following chart illustrates the environmental influences of "then and there" and "here and now."

CHART OF ENVIRONMENTAL INFLUENCES

BOOK	SETTING	POPULATIONS	BASIC HUMAN NEEDS
LIST	DESCRIBE	IDENTIFY/ DESCRIBE	DESCRIBE HOW EACH IS FULFILLED
title, author	climate	frontier	food
characters	land forms	rural	clothing
location	environ- ment	town	shelter
		city	love

Complete the data on this chart for each book to be compared. Then complete the data based on the lives of the children here and now. The data may be used to compare the environmental influences of setting of several books with one another and with the lives of the children, here and now.

Add Pictures and Words to the Chart: The chart may be filled with words and/or pictures that show the influence of the environment. The words may take the form of a **glossary of terms** that were used in another time and another region, but are not used by children today. Other data may be drawn from the content of the children's books.

Writing About Another Time/Another Place: As a follow-up activity, children can write, draw or tell about their lives and the characters' lives as **"A Day in the Life of . . . ."** This language activity will identify how their lives and the characters' lives are alike and different because of the environment in which they live and the influences of technologies in their lives.

Mural: Then and There, Here and Now. The same data may be shown as a mural of "then and there" and "here and now." Include appropriate **labels such as names, dates, and locations.** Both the **chart** and the **mural** lead into and are important components of the concepts about multicultural peoples.

∞∞∞∞∞∞∞∞∞∞∞∞∞∞

DEVELOPING THE CONCEPT OF MULTICULTURAL PEOPLES

TO BEGIN: Self-Awareness Activities. Pursue several self-awareness activities with the children, about themselves, then do the same activities from the viewpoint of the book characters. These activities could be **self-portraits, biographical poems, sentence starters,** and other writing and drawing tasks that focus on the **physical, emotional, and intellectual characteristics** of the children and the book characters. Encourage children to represent the **racial and ethnic characteristics** for themselves and for the book characters. It will be difficult to stereotype their own characteristics or those of the book characters when participating in the same self-awareness activities for themselves and for the characters.

Self-portraits are appropriate for both early and later elementary children. Ask children to draw themselves participating in their favorite activity, doing their household chores, attending school, or going somewhere with their best friend. Include the settings, appropriate clothing, equipment, or appliances. Then draw a parallel portrait of the book character showing a parallel setting. Other self-portraits could include family members and other people important to children and to the book characters. **The self-portraits may be part of the mural.**

Sentence starters will encourage children to write about themselves and the book characters. Ask children to complete some of the following sentence starters about themselves, and then about the book characters. This **self-awareness writing activity** may be helpful in identifying viewpoints, values, and beliefs of the past and the present.

1. The most beautiful sight I ever saw was when I. . . .
2. I had so much fun when I. . . .
3. I laughed and laughed when. . . .
4. I was proud of myself when I. . . .
5. I was proud of my friends/siblings/family when. . . .
6. It took all the courage I had to. . . .
7. _____ was so brave when she/he . . . .
8. My favorite possession is. . . .
9. The people I love the most are. . . .
10. I try to be truthful because. . . .
11. I am usually brave, but I get scared when. . . .
12. I do not like it when other people call me. . . .
13. I really get angry when. . . .
14. I am sad when. . . .
15. I can be kind to other people by. . . .
16. What I like best in other people is. . . .
17. My best friend is. . . .

ETHNICITY, RACE, AND NATIONAL ORIGINS

The **outline map, time line, charts,** and **mural** will provide the foundations for identifying the diversity among the peoples of the past and the present. The **self-awareness activities** establish the varied personal identities of the children and of the book characters. Differences among children and among the book characters will be well-defined through the sequence of activities leading into this section and will be further clarified through the following activities.

Family Origins: Sharing the information about family origins from various regions of the United States and of the world will acknowledge and place value upon the diversity among Americans. Assist children in finding books about people with their own family's national origins, such as the

Polish immigrants in *First Farm in the Valley* by Anne Pellowski, or the Chinese people in Laurence Yep's *Dragonwings*. To establish a sense of "roots," a variety of sources of information about the regions of the United States or other nations should be available for children.

Ethnic Customs Related to Basic Human Needs: Based on the children's literature and other sources of information including family members, list customs, celebrations, foods, songs, and games associated with the specific ethnic groups represented in the literature and the classroom. Involve parents as resource speakers about their families' customs, both past and present. List these cultural and ethnic practices under the headings of basic human needs: food, clothing, shelter, love. Children will discover that diversity among people is evident in the history of America as well as today.

Interview Questions may be developed to use with parents and other adults, leading children to become researchers about their origins and the origins of others. Interview questions may also then be applied to the book characters, giving another dimension to understanding the diversity of American peoples. Interview questions should seek to identify both likenesses and differences among people, such as:

1. My family is similar to other families because. . . .
2. My family is different from other families because. . . .
3. In my family, we like to. . . .
4. For a special treat, my family likes to eat. . . .
5. Something that I have learned from my family is. . . .

COMPARING CHILDREN'S LIVES, PAST AND PRESENT

Children's Tasks, Past and Present: To further emphasize the concept that history includes the commonplace people including children, list the jobs and responsibilities of today's children and compare with children of the past through information drawn from the children's books. The comparisons of present-day children with children of the past may lead to the conclusions that today's children have few responsibilities and many advantages.

Children's Decisions, Past and Present: Depending on the grade level of the children, extend the comparisons to include the decisions children make today and in the past; levels of education; and potential jobs and careers for girls and boys. These topics may be pursued in depth by middle school youngsters. For young children, a few examples may help children identify that their responsibilities are different, although not necessarily less significant.

Children's Responsibilities: Children's responsibilities of today could be compared with children's responsibilities in the some of the following situations drawn from children's books:

Immigration from Europe or Asia, or When My Family Moved to a New Home (cite dates, countries or ethnic origins and destination).

Life in a Native American Home, or Life in My Home Today (cite specific tribe, location, and time frame).

On the Trail Westward, or When My Family Went Camping, or Traveled to Another Place (cite trail, place of origin, destination, and date).

On the Homestead, or How I Help My Family Maintain Our Home (cite date, location of home, and origin of family).

Early Days of a Settlement, or How I Use the Resources of My Community (cite location, date, origin of family, and resources of the settlement or community).

Other headings may be drawn from specific books. Children will discover that their lives and responsibilities are different from the children of another time and place because of the changes in technologies, in the environment, and in some cases, beliefs and values.

∞∞∞∞∞∞∞∞∞∞∞∞∞

WRITING AND DRAWING ACTIVITIES

Through writing and drawing learning activities, children will come to understand that people of other times and places also had thoughts, ideas, and values that are both similar and different from those of children today. For example:

1.   Write additional adventures of a book character in which the character faces fear, has fun or expresses humor, is kind to others, or expresses love and respect for their family or their ethnic group.

2.   Write and illustrate poems that convey the immigrants' reasons for leaving their homelands and their joys and sorrows in the new land.

3.   Write and illustrate poems that describe the Native American reverence for the land, animals, plants, family, and tribal life.

4.   Write and illustrate personal journals about immigration, the wagon train journey, early days of homesteading, or living in an early-day community.

5.   Illustrate the events from the children's books in which the main characters are in conflict with people from another culture.

6.   Design posters and newspaper advertisements for various trails west. State the advantages of the trail and of homesteading land.

7.   Advertise the railroad and telegraph and their advantages.

8.   Select portions of children's books for readers' theater.

∞∞∞∞∞∞∞∞∞∞∞∞∞

THE ROLE OF TEACHERS, LIBRARIANS, AND PARENTS

As with all the learning experiences listed, the teacher, parent, or librarian should select those most appropriate for individuals and for groups, suitable to the age and learning level of the children, and appropriate to the historical setting and people of the literature. To attempt to pursue all the learning activities with any single book or time frame may produce the detrimental effect of driving children away from their historical heritage.

In helping children understand themselves and others, both past and present, the concept of being different loses the pejorative implications as children gain in experience and comprehension of other times, other places, and other peoples. Through children's realistic historical literature, today's children can begin to vicariously experience portions of their heritage. With help from parents, teachers, and librarians, the stereotypes of the American West can be replaced with realistic historical perspectives about place, time, change, and people. These learning experiences beyond the basal social studies textbook establish for children the reality of the diversity of America's heritage through the exploration of the other times and lives found in realistic historical children's literature.

∞∞∞∞∞∞∞∞∞∞∞∞∞∞

NOTES

All books cited in this chapter will be found in the bibliography.

1 Russell Freedman, *Indian Chiefs* (New York: Holiday House, 1987), 4.

2 Timeliner Rel. 1986, Tom Synder Productions, Cambridge, MA.

The Selected, Annotated Bibliography

In the bibliography the annotations of the books are arranged by main topic, grade level, and are in alphabetical order by author. Although there are relatively few books at the early elementary level, please note the many possibilities for read-aloud books among the books at higher reading levels.

The readability levels are indicated by the following abbreviations: BOR: Bormuth Readability Index Formula; FLE: Flesch Scale of Readability; FOG: Fog Index of Printed Materials; and FRY: Fry Readability Formula.

∞∞∞∞∞∞∞∞∞∞∞∞∞∞∞

Homesteading and Settling in the West

GRADES K-3

BOOK TITLE: **LITTLE YELLOW FUR**
AUTHOR: Wilma Pitchford Hays
PUBLISHER: Coward, McCann & Geoghegan, Inc., 1973
ILLUSTRATOR: Richard Cuffari
FICTION
ISBN: SBN TR-689-20250-3

READABILITY LEVEL: BOR: 3.8/ FLE: 1.0/ FOG: 6.1/ FRY: 4.0
DESCRIPTORS:

> Geographic Location: South Dakota, near the Rosebud Indian Reservation
> Dates: 1913
> Main Characters (race, sex, age, nationality)
>> Susanna (white, female, approx. 6 yrs. old, American)
>> Mama and Papa (white, approx. 30 yrs. old, American)
>> Red Cloud (Sioux Indian, male, approx. 60 yrs. old)

SYNOPSIS:
This book is a series of five stories, divided into chapters, based on the author's recollections of her girlhood spent homesteading with her parents in the "wild country" of South Dakota around 1913. The homestead was very close to the Rosebud Indian Reservation where Susanna makes friends with some of the Sioux Indians. Susanna's mother is afraid of the Indians, especially the day that some young men ride up to the house. Mama barricades Susanna and herself in the house while the men laugh and call out to them. They are being mischievous and do not really intend any harm, but Mama does

not see it that way. Red Cloud, an old Sioux Indian Chief, explains to Papa how dramatically the Indian way of life changed since they were herded onto reservations and that the young men are bored without the great prairies to hunt on. Susanna, nicknamed "Little Yellow Fur" by the Indians because of her blonde hair, visits the reservation and gets to know the Indians and even some Sioux words. The Indian women make a Sioux dress and a pair of moccasins for her and in the end, even Mama realizes that the Indians are simply people like themselves and she loses some of her hostilities towards them.

ILLUSTRATIONS:
The book has simple illustrations, some in black and white and some in color, which help illustrate for young readers what the author is saying. Both the white and Native American ways of life are portrayed in the pictures.

STRENGTHS OF BOOK:
One of the book's strengths is that it is based on the author's experiences homesteading in the early twentieth century. It is interesting to note that even in the present century, living on the prairie was still a difficult and stressful existence. The low reading level makes this an excellent book for primary readers and it will appeal to both sexes.

CONTENT FOR FURTHER DEVELOPMENT:
The most obvious topic for further discussion is how the Indians perceived the coming of the white people, as voiced by Red Cloud, and how this altered the Indian way of life. Mama's fear of the Indians could be discussed--a natural reaction about the unknown.

∞∞∞∞∞∞∞∞∞∞∞∞∞∞

BOOK TITLE: **YELLOW FUR AND LITTLE HAWK**
AUTHOR: Wilma Pitchford Hays
PUBLISHER: Coward, McCann & Geoghegan, Inc., 1980
ILLUSTRATOR: Anthony Rao

FICTION
ISBN: 0-698-30687-2

READABILITY LEVEL: BOR: 4.1/ FLE: 4.0/ FOG: 6.6/ FRY: 5.3
DESCRIPTORS:
Geographic Location: South Dakota, near Sioux Indian
    Reservation
Dates: 1915
Main Characters (race, sex, age, nationality)
    Susanna (white, female, approx. 8 yrs. old, American)
    Little Hawk (Sioux Indian, male, approx. 9 yrs. old)
    Mama and Papa (white, approx. 30s, American)

SYNOPSIS:
In this sequel to *Little Yellow Fur*, Susanna is now two years
older and living through the drought of the summer of 1915. As
the book opens, Susanna's father is putting the finishing touches
on some houses he has been commissioned to build for the
Indians on the nearby Sioux Reservation. However, the Sioux
do not want to live in square houses, as the holy man White
Bull explains to Susanna, because nature orders that they live in
circular homes such as tipis. A frequent visitor to the Sioux
village, Susanna, or "Yellow Fur" as the Indians call her, spends
much time with her friend, Little Hawk. Together they watch
the jester-like Heyokas cavorting in the village and learn about
Sioux ways. When their creek dries up because of the drought,
Susanna's family travels to a nearby river, bringing water back
which they share with the Indians. The family comes home to
find Susanna's dog, Terk, missing and with the help of the Sioux
they find him nearly dehydrated but still alive. The book
culminates with a hailstorm that inadvertently solves the
problem of the Indians' housing arrangements.

ILLUSTRATIONS:
Both the color and black-and-white drawings enhance the text
and help picture the occurrences in the story. Scenes from the
white and Indian cultures are included.

STRENGTHS OF BOOK:
Wilma Pitchford Hays spent the early years of her childhood as a homesteader in South Dakota and Susanna's story is based largely on the author's experiences and memories.   The differences between the Native American and white ways of life are sensitively presented in a manner which younger children will clearly comprehend. This story is suitable for reading aloud.

CONTENT FOR FURTHER DEVELOPMENT:
This story shows the Indians having to conform to the white people's ways, for example, by having to live in wooden houses with doors and windows. The difficulties experienced by Native Americans as they tried to adapt to new ways should be discussed. The Indians and whites cooperated in this story and it should be pointed out that in many instances, both peoples succeeded in being close neighbors.

∞∞∞∞∞∞∞∞∞∞∞∞∞

GRADES 4-9

BOOK TITLE: **A LANTERN IN HER HAND**
AUTHOR: Bess Streeter Aldrich
PUBLISHER: Grosset & Dunlap, 1928
FICTION
ISBN: None

READABILITY LEVEL: BOR: 6.4/ FLE: 9.5/ FOG: 12.9/ FRY: 10.0
DESCRIPTORS:
   Geographic Location: Blackhawk County, IA and Cedartown, NE
   Dates: 1854-1930
   Main Characters (race, sex, age, nationality)
      Abbie Mackenzie Deal (white, female, 18-80 yrs. old, Scottish heritage)
      Will Deal (white, male, approx. early 20s, American)

Mack, Margaret, John, Isabelle and Grace Deal (their children)

SYNOPSIS:
In 1854, when Abbie Mackenzie is eight years old, she and her family travel from Illinois to Iowa. At age nineteen Abbie marries Will Deal and they move to Nebraska to settle with three other families in an area that comes to be known as Cedartown. Two of the families are from Michigan and the other couple is from Sweden. Abbie and Will's family continues to grow as they live in a sod house. Drought prevails for about thirteen years, but eventually the land begins to produce more and they build a real house. The town of Cedartown begins to flourish and as the Deal children mature, they leave the family home and go their separate ways. Ultimately Will dies and Abbie elects to remain in her house. At the age of eighty-four Abbie dies in the home that she and her husband built.

ILLUSTRATIONS: None

STRENGTHS OF BOOK:
This book covers a large span of time during which much growth and development occurs. The barren area where Abbie and Will settled becomes a thriving city. Abbie is continually thinking back to how it was when she and her husband came to Nebraska and comparing it to the present.

CONTENT FOR FURTHER DEVELOPMENT:
A thirteen-year-old drought is a serious matter and it might be interesting to find out how other settlers handled this trying situation.

∞∞∞∞∞∞∞∞∞∞∞∞∞∞

BOOK TITLE: **THAT'S ONE ORNERY ORPHAN**
AUTHOR: Patricia Beatty
PUBLISHER: William Morrow & Co., 1980
FICTION
ISBN: 0-688-22227-7

READABILITY LEVEL: BOR: 5.2/ FLE: 6.0/ FOG: 8.2/ FRY: 6.0
DESCRIPTORS:
   Geographic Location: Blanco County, TX
   Dates: 1889
   Main Characters (race, sex, age, nationality)
      Hallie Lee Baker (white, female, 13 yrs. old, American)
      C.T. Hopkins (white, female, approx. 40s, American)
      Maybell Duff (white, female, 16 yrs. old, American)

SYNOPSIS:
Hallie is taken to an orphanage, operated by C.T. Hopkins, following the death of her grandfather, who was Hallie's legal guardian. Her habit for telling tall tales about herself gets Hallie into many less-than-desirable situations. Her experiences with the various foster families that take her home include a preacher and his family, a doctor, a theater woman, and finally, an immigrant German family that adopts her as a daughter rather than treating her like a hired hand. The author's note at the end explains that many of Hallie's feelings towards farmers and several of her escapades, such as the camp meetings and mixing up the babies, are based upon facts.

ILLUSTRATIONS: None

STRENGTHS OF BOOK:
The book's humor is one of its strengths and it will probably have great appeal for female readers. The story touches upon some aspects of pioneer life that are not usually included in children's literature such as intermarriage between families, religious camp meetings, and the patent medicine business.

CONTENT FOR FURTHER DEVELOPMENT:
The reasons behind Hallie's practice of fibbing and fabricating stories may need to be explored. Has the lot of orphans changed much from the last century?

∞∞∞∞∞∞∞∞∞∞∞∞∞∞∞

BOOK TITLE: **THE SNOWBIRD**
AUTHOR: Patricia Calvert
PUBLISHER: Scribner's, 1980
FICTION
ISBN: 0-684-16719-0

READABILITY LEVEL: BOR: 7.2/ FLE: 7.5/ FOG: 12.4/ FRY: 8.0
DESCRIPTORS:
Geographic Location: Tennessee to Dakota Territory
Dates: 1883
Main Characters (race, sex, age, nationality)
Willanna (white, female, 14 yrs. old, American)
T.J. (white, male, 6 yrs. old, American)
Belle and Randall Bannerman (white, approx. 40 yrs.
old, Irish heritage)

SYNOPSIS:
The story opens when Willanna and T.J.'s parents are killed in a
fire in their Tennessee home. The two children then travel to
the Red River area in the Dakota Territory to live with their
aunt and uncle, whom they have never met. Willanna
experiences the typical adolescent problems of wondering who
she is and what will become of her, but these are complicated by
the sudden loss of her parents. Willanna and T.J. learn about
the hardships and loneliness of life on the prairie, and Willanna
gains comfort from her beloved horse, Snowbird. Willanna and
T.J. attend school in the town nearby and become friends with
some of their classmates, including some immigrant children
from Finland. After her Aunt Belle leaves the family, Willanna
eventually comes to grips with her own destiny.

ILLUSTRATIONS: None

STRENGTHS OF BOOK:
The book is poetically written and illustrates how prairie life was
unbearable for some people and that not everyone succeeded in
their farming endeavors.

CONTENT FOR FURTHER DEVELOPMENT:
The reasons behind Aunt Belle's departure might be discussed.
Were her feelings shared by other people trying to homestead on
the prairie?

∞∞∞∞∞∞∞∞∞∞∞∞

BOOK TITLE: **FRONTIER FARMER: KANSAS ADVENTURES**
AUTHOR: Catherine E. Chambers
PUBLISHER: Troll Associates, 1984 (Adventures in Frontier
            America Series)
ILLUSTRATOR: Len Epstein
FICTION
ISBN: 0-8167-0053-2

READABILITY LEVEL: BOR: 4.0/ FLE: 3.8/ FOG: 6.2/ FRY: 3.3
DESCRIPTORS:
    Geographic Location: Kansas
    Dates: 1881-84
    Main Characters (race, sex, age, nationality)
        Matt Foster (white, male, 13 yrs. old, American)
        Mrs. Foster (white, female, late 30s, American)
        William Lee (black, male, late 30s, American)
        Abraham Lee (black, male, 13 yrs. old, American)

SYNOPSIS:
Thirteen-year-old Matt Foster and his mother decide to remain
in Kansas and work their homestead despite the death of Mr.
Foster. Subsequently, Mrs. Foster places an advertisement in the
newspaper for a farmer to help them. William Lee, who was
born a field slave in Virginia, responds to her inquiry and brings
his son, Abraham, with him to live with the Fosters. There are
problems with ranchers cutting the Fosters' fences so that their
cattle can get through. The Fosters and the Lees eventually catch
the "nightriders" doing the damage. Some of the townspeople
feel that it is necessary to hang the criminals, but Mrs. Foster
convinces them to leave that decision to a jury. After a while,

Mr. Lee is able to homestead some land near the Foster's and in June 1884, Matt and his mother acquire ownership of the land.

ILLUSTRATIONS:
Black-and-white ink drawings depict the action in the story and the blacks are portrayed realistically.

STRENGTHS OF BOOK:
The book includes minority characters who are treated as equals. It also speaks to the problems between farmers and ranchers, which were common at that time. This story is available as a spoken recording.

CONTENT FOR FURTHER DEVELOPMENT:
While the book does address the conflicts between farmers and ranchers, it does not explain how those problems were resolved. Children may want to research and discuss how farmers and ranchers dealt with their differences. The use of guns and the near-hanging in the story should also be talked about. How do we handle the types of problems presented in the story today? Such legendary characters and places as Wild Bill Hickock, Buffalo Bill, nightriders, and Dodge City are mentioned in the story and students might want to learn more about them. Another title in the Adventures in Frontier America Series by Catherine E. Chambers is *Frontier Village: A Town Is Born* (Troll Associates, 1984).

∞∞∞∞∞∞∞∞∞∞∞∞∞

BOOK TITLE: **PRAIRIE SONGS**
AUTHOR: Pam Conrad
PUBLISHER: Harper and Row, 1985
ILLUSTRATOR: Darryl S. Zudeck
FICTION
ISBN: 0-06-021336-1

READABILITY LEVEL: BOR: 5.0/ FLE: 6.2/ FOG: 6.9/ FRY: 5.7
DESCRIPTORS:
   Geographic Location: Howard County, NE
   Dates: Late 1800s

Main Characters (race, sex, age, nationality)
    Louisa Downing (white, female, 11 or 12 yrs. old,
        American)
    Lester Downing (white, male, 6-8 yrs. old, American)
    Clara and J.T. Downing (white, 40-50 yrs. old, American)
    Emmeline and William Berryman (white, late 20s,
        American)

SYNOPSIS:
Louisa Downing has lived on the prairie since birth. Although she describes the prairie as a "lonely land," she sees it as a nice kind of lonely. The Downings and their neighbors, the Whitfields, are happy when a doctor and his wife, William and Emmeline Berryman, move into the nearest soddy, or sod house. Emmeline gives reading lessons to Louisa and her brother, Lester, who is painfully shy and speaks only to his family. As Lester begins to open up around others, Emmeline begins to fade into a world of her own, especially after her baby dies. The prairie, which is such a beautiful, song-filled world for Louisa, is not so for Emmeline as she gradually loses her will to survive.

ILLUSTRATIONS:
Includes a few pencil drawings with very soft lines that give a sense of serenity.

STRENGTHS OF BOOK:
The story is written poetically and contains good imagery. It illustrates the various ways prairie life affected the settlers.

CONTENT FOR FURTHER DEVELOPMENT:
Native Americans are portrayed only as people who come to the house, demand to be fed, do not smell good, and take the family's horse. The Indians' reaction to a picture of Christ on the cross may warrant some discussion. The psychological and physical effect of the prairie's desolation on its inhabitants might be further investigated.

∞∞∞∞∞∞∞∞∞∞∞∞∞∞∞

BOOK TITLE: **THE THUNDERING PRAIRIE**
AUTHOR: Mary A. Hancock
PUBLISHER: Macrae Smith Co., 1969
ILLUSTRATOR: H. Tom Hall
FICTION
ISBN: None

READABILITY LEVEL: BOR: 5.6/ FLE: 6.0/ FOG: 8.9/ FRY: 6.0
DESCRIPTORS:
   Geographic Location: Eastern Kentucky to Cherokee Strip,
      Oklahoma Territory
   Dates: 1893
   Main Characters (race, sex, age, nationality)
      Benjy Bryan (white, male, 14 yrs. old, American)
      Joel Bryan (white, male, 17 yrs. old, American)
      Sue Bryan (white, female, 16 yrs. old, American)
      Mrs. Bryan (white, female, approx. 40s, American)

SYNOPSIS:
This book is based on the recollections of people who
participated in the land runs of the late nineteenth century.
While Mr. Bryan remains hospitalized from a mining accident,
the rest of the family travels by wagon from Kentucky to the
Oklahoma Territory to take part in the land run in the Cherokee
Strip on September 16, 1893. The family encounters a horse thief
and a prairie fire on their journey, but are helped out of both
catastrophes by the Tabor family, whom they meet along the
way. Once they are camped near the starting line, Joel and his
horse are injured so that Benjy and his mule are forced to make
the run along with his mother. When it seems as if the Bryans
are not going to get a claim staked, Benjy runs across the horse
thief who illegally claimed his land before the proper time.
With the assistance of Mr. Tabor, Benjy captures the wily thief,
claims the land, and receives a $200 reward.

ILLUSTRATIONS:
Small ink drawings mark the beginning of each chapter.

STRENGTHS OF BOOK:
This book will interest both boys and girls. Land runs were very exciting and extraordinary events and the book's readers will enjoy learning about this phenomenal aspect of the development of the West which is not commonly covered in children's books.

CONTENT FOR FURTHER DEVELOPMENT:
The Homestead Act of 1862 will need further discussion, as will the various reasons why Americans sacrificed so much in order to own their own land. The Indian policy of relocation onto reservations might be another topic for development. Was it right and/or fair for the government to force the Indians to leave their homelands in order to give that land away to white settlers? Native Americans are still fighting today to regain their lands and it would be enlightening to investigate what the current federal policy is regarding this issue.

∞∞∞∞∞∞∞∞∞∞∞∞∞

BOOK TITLE: **MY PRAIRIE YEAR: BASED ON THE DIARY OF ELENORE PLAISTED**
AUTHOR: Brett Harvey
PUBLISHER: Holiday House, 1986
ILLUSTRATOR: Deborah Kogan Ray
FICTION
ISBN: 0-8234-0604-0

READABILITY LEVEL: BOR: 5.9/ FLE: 7.0/ FOG: 8.7/ FRY: 7.3
DESCRIPTORS:
    Geographic Location: Dakota Territory
    Dates: 1889-90
    Main Characters (race, sex, age, nationality)
        Elenore Plaisted (white, female, 9 yrs. old, American)
        Various members of the Plaisted family

SYNOPSIS:
This book is based on the reminiscences of Elenore Plaisted, and
it vividly depicts the everyday life of Dakota homesteaders--
women, men, and children. In 1889 the Plaisted family left their
home in Lincoln, Maine, and traveled by railroad to farm in the
Dakotas. The special chores of each day, for example, washing
on Monday and baking on Saturday, include descriptions of how
the children's work was important to the family's subsistence.
As the oldest of three children, Elenore had many
responsibilities, including the care of her younger siblings. The
value placed on education is evidenced in Mother's teaching the
children at home because there is no school nearby. The seasons
of the year for a rural family include both hard labor as well as
recreation, surviving a tornado and a prairie fire, and bring the
realization that they are now at home on the plains.

ILLUSTRATIONS:
The soft charcoal drawings, almost impressionistic in style, add
depth and interest to the story.

STRENGTHS OF BOOK:
Family unity is strong in this book and children are seen as
integral and productive members in establishing the family's
new home. The story is based on the writings of Brett Harvey's
grandmother, Elenore Plaisted, who became a successful
illustrator of children's books. Between grandmother and
grandson, the imagery in *My Prairie Year* is a work of art.

CONTENT FOR FURTHER DEVELOPMENT:
It might be interesting to compare the life of pioneer children
with that of children today. Do today's children have certain
chores they must complete in the household? Are they
compensated monetarily?

∞∞∞∞∞∞∞∞∞∞∞∞∞∞

BOOK TITLE: **FACING THE ENEMY**
AUTHOR: Dean Hughes
PUBLISHER: Deseret Book Company, 1982

FICTION
ISBN: 0-87747-928-3

READABILITY LEVEL: BOR: 4.0/ FLE: 6.0/ FOG: 7.2/ FRY: 5.0
DESCRIPTORS:
Geographic Location: Northern Missouri, cities of Far West
and Haun's Mill
Dates: Late 1830s
Main Characters (race, sex, age, nationality)
Joseph Williams (white, male 16 yrs. old, American)
Matthew Williams (white, male, 18 yrs. old, American)
Various members of the Williams family

SYNOPSIS:
After fleeing their home in Jackson County, Missouri, because of
anti-Mormon sentiment, the Williams family relocates in the
Mormon community of Far West. Mr. Williams was slain in an
attack on the Mormons and now it is up to young Matthew to
keep the family together. The story is told from the perspective
of his younger brother, Joseph, a teenager who is encountering
difficulty in reconciling the hostilities taking place. The various
Mormon communities in northern Missouri are still disliked by
the "old settlers," the non-Mormons who were established in
the towns when the Mormons arrived, and Joseph gradually
becomes involved in transporting messages between the
Mormon towns. After the Mormon inhabitants of DeWitt are
forced to leave their homes, the Williams family takes in a
homeless family, and later on a second family--a total of
seventeen people in a one-room cabin. Joseph is sickened by the
destruction, death and violence being perpetrated by the old
settlers and when he learns that the Mormons have been
inflicting some of the same, his faith in the Mormon value
system is badly shaken. This is the story of an unfortunate
chapter in the history of the American West, as well as the tale
of a young man's coming of age. *Under the Same Stars* (Deseret
Book Co., 1979), also written by Dean Hughes, precedes *Facing
the Enemy*.

ILLUSTRATIONS:
A detailed map is included outlining the various towns that
Joseph visited and the exodus of the Mormons from Missouri to
Quincy, Illinois.

STRENGTHS OF BOOK:
This is a realistic portrayal of the religious intolerance
experienced by Mormons in our nation's early history. The story
is sensitively written and the characterizations are well-drawn.
In the process of Joseph's self-examination, the reader is allowed
to see both sides of the issue and this book will appeal to both
male and female readers.

CONTENT FOR FURTHER DEVELOPMENT:
The obvious conflict between religious intolerance and the
principles on which the United States was founded is an
excellent topic for further study. Students may want to learn
more about the Mormon religion and why the old settlers were
so threatened by these hard-working, responsible citizens.
Brigham Young emerges in this story as a Mormon leader and a
good follow-up might be to trace the movement of the
Mormons from the Midwest to Utah.

∞∞∞∞∞∞∞∞∞∞∞∞∞∞

BOOK TITLE: **LET THE HURRICANE ROAR**
AUTHOR: Rose Wilder Lane
PUBLISHER: Longmans, Green and Company, 1933
FICTION
ISBN: None

READABILITY LEVEL: BOR: 5.0/ FLE: 5.0/ FOG: 7.3/ FRY: 5.0
DESCRIPTORS:
    Geographic Location: Dakota Territory
    Dates: Middle to late 1800s
    Main Characters (race, sex, age, nationality)
        Caroline (white, female, 16 yrs. old, American)
        Charles (white, male, 19 yrs. old, American)

SYNOPSIS:
Following their wedding, Charles and Caroline leave their families to travel to the Dakotas. Charles works on the railroad for a while to earn money. Before winter sets in they claim some land and move into a dugout along Wild Plum Creek. Caroline has her first baby, Charles John, on her seventeenth birthday. Swedish neighbors move in about a half a mile away. During the summer they have a good crop until grasshoppers come and destroy their harvest. Leaving Caroline and the baby, Charles goes to the East to find work so that he might pay off a debt. Caroline spends the winter alone because Charles is unable to make it back before the bad weather sets in and their neighbors are forced to move back to Minnesota.

ILLUSTRATIONS: None

STRENGTHS OF BOOK:
In this book, the author presents a vivid description of the difficulties encountered in homesteading, and that sometimes people failed in their endeavors regardless of their efforts.

CONTENT FOR FURTHER DEVELOPMENT:
Because no explanation is given, there may be some question as to how a dugout is made. Research into the subject may be a good way to begin a study on different kinds of shelters used in the West.

∞∞∞∞∞∞∞∞∞∞∞∞∞∞

BOOK TITLE: **ADDIE ACROSS THE PRAIRIE**
AUTHOR: Laurie Lawlor
PUBLISHER: Albert Whitman & Co., 1986
ILLUSTRATOR: Gail Owens
FICTION
ISBN: 0-8075-0165-4

READABILITY LEVEL: BOR: 5.5/ FLE: 6.0/ FOG: 7.9/ FRY: 6.0
DESCRIPTORS:
    Geographic Location: Iowa to the Dakota Territory

Dates: 1883
Main Characters (race, sex, age, nationality)
    Addie Mills (white, female, 9 yrs. old, American)
    George Mills (white, male, 8 yrs. old, American)
    Becca and Samuel Mills (white, approx. 30s, American)

SYNOPSIS:
Addie Mills is not happy when her parents decide to leave their
comfortable farm in Iowa to homestead in the Dakotas. But this
is an opportunity for the Mills' to own land and so in the fall of
1883 the family departs on their 500-mile trek, leaving behind
family and friends. Unlike many other books of this genre, the
story does not concentrate on the rigors of the wagon trip, but
rather on conditions once the family reaches their Oak Hollow
homestead. As the oldest of five children, much of the
responsibility for helping her mother and watching the younger
children falls to Addie. Once the Mills arrive in Dakota they live
for a while with a couple named Fency whose hospitality is
gratefully appreciated. Addie thinks the sod house, or soddy, is a
poor comparison to the two-story frame house back in Iowa.
Much of the story is told from her viewpoint and the reader gets
a clear picture of how difficult homesteading was on children.
Not only does Addie not have much time for play, but she also
worries about "grownup" matters such as locust attacks, Indians,
and brush fires. Even though a child, she feels the great
isolation of the prairie and laments that there are no other
houses or chimneys in sight. Addie does not feel she is the
"sodbusting pioneer type," but by the end of the story she proves
this to be otherwise in a series of harrowing experiences,
including a surprise visit from some Indians and a prairie blaze.

ILLUSTRATIONS:
There are simple black-and-white drawings scattered throughout
the text which help to visualize the action and conditions of
homesteading on the northern plains.

STRENGTHS OF BOOK:
This is a well-written and interesting story that maintains the
reader's interest. It does an admirable job of representing

pioneers who uprooted themselves from their settled homes in order to move west and farm their own land.

CONTENT FOR FURTHER DEVELOPMENT:
The quest for free land is a concept for additional study. The responsibilities assigned to young children should prove an interesting discussion topic, especially in comparison to today's children. Several times the book mentions the Sioux Indians on the reservations, and the pitiful condition of the Indians who visit the Fency homestead should not be overlooked.

∞∞∞∞∞∞∞∞∞∞∞∞∞∞

BOOK TITLE: **SARAH, PLAIN AND TALL**
AUTHOR: Patricia MacLachlan
PUBLISHER: Harper & Row, 1985
FICTION
ISBN: 0-06-024101-2

READABILITY LEVEL: BOR: 4.5/ FLE: 5.0/ FOG: 6.2/ FRY: 5.0
DESCRIPTORS:
    Geographic Location: Small town in American West
    Dates: Late 1800s
    Main Characters (race, sex, age, nationality)
        Anna (white, female, approx. 8 yrs. old, American)
        Papa (white, male, late 30s, American)
        Sarah Wheaton (white, female, approx. 30s, American)

SYNOPSIS:
Papa places an advertisement in a newspaper out East for a wife because he feels his two children, Anna and Caleb, need a mother and because he is lonely. Mama died in childbirth some time before, and now Papa does not sing anymore. The advertisement is answered by a woman named Sarah Wheaton who lives in Maine. The children want a mother very much and they eagerly and worriedly await her coming. Sarah arrives in the spring with her cat, Seal. Although the family likes her, they are concerned she will leave because she seems homesick and misses the green landscape of Maine and the blue ocean.

However, in time Sarah grows to love Papa, Anna, and Caleb and she decides to remain and complete their family unit.

ILLUSTRATIONS: None

STRENGTHS OF BOOK:
This Newbery-award-winning book depicts Sarah as more than just the traditional wife, cook, and housekeeper. It shows Sarah as an integral part of the family, fixing the roof and driving the wagon, and also displays her more feminine nature as evidenced by her care of the family, farm animals, and her beloved garden. The author uses descriptive and colorful language to convey both the beauty and isolation of the prairie. This story is available as a spoken recording.

CONTENT FOR FURTHER DEVELOPMENT:
The whole question of mail-order brides should spur some discussion. It not only demonstrates the importance of women in the development of the West, but also makes a statement about the women who left their settled homes to choose marriage and adventure. Sarah comes to live with the family on a month's trial basis, allowing her and Papa to develop a relationship before the marriage. It is very probable that many mail-order brides were not as lucky as Sarah.

∞∞∞∞∞∞∞∞∞∞∞∞∞

BOOK TITLE: **MOCCASIN TRAIL**
AUTHOR: Eloise Jarvis McGraw
PUBLISHER: Coward-McCann, 1952
FICTION
ISBN: None

READABILITY LEVEL: BOR: 5.1/ FLE: 6.0/ FOG: 7.3/ FRY: 6.0
DESCRIPTORS:
    Geographic Location: Oregon Territory
    Dates: 1844-45
    Main Characters (race, sex, age, nationality)
        Jim Keath (white, male, 18 yrs. old, American)

Jonathan Keath (white, male, approx. 17 yrs. old,
   American)
Sally Keath (white, female, 15 yrs. old, American)
Daniel Keath (white, male, 11 yrs. old, American)

SYNOPSIS:
When he is eleven, Jim Keath runs away from his family's
Missouri homestead to be a trapper with his uncle in far-away
Oregon. One day a grizzly bear attacks the trappers' camp and
Jim is left for dead. A tribe of Crow Indians nurses him back to
health and he remains with them for six years, earning both an
Indian name, Talks Alone, and the right to wear the signs of
Indian manhood. He learns how to pull a bow, dance, steal
horses, hunt, stalk--in essence, to survive. In his own mind he
has become a Crow and when at age eighteen he receives a letter
from his brother, Jonathan, asking Jim to come back to claim the
family's homestead in Oregon, Jim is in a quandary. He is
caught between his more recent Crow life and the vague
memories of life as a white boy. He does go and help his family
and they are dismayed to see an Indian instead of their brother,
wearing the trappings of braids, feathers, and moccasins. For
many months Jim feels more Crow than Keath and he has a
difficult time understanding why the whites want to tame the
country and why they want to sleep in cabins. After several
adventures Jim finally comes to grips with his dilemma and is
able to resolve his feelings.

ILLUSTRATIONS: None

STRENGTHS OF BOOK:
The story is a vivid depiction of the day-to-day existence of the
early settlers, beginning with having to clear the woods, cut the
timber for the log houses, build the cabins, and clear the land for
the fields. The reader gets a real sense of the hardships that faced
the pioneers, but also the tremendous rewards. This book is
available as a spoken recording.

CONTENT FOR FURTHER DEVELOPMENT:
The predominant topic for further study is the clash of the Indian and white cultures and the conflicts that Jim felt, torn between the two. He feels the whites will ruin the beautiful forest and valleys, cutting down trees and scaring away the game. In his own words the settlers want to "...tame it and plow it and fill it with people." (p. 94.)

∞∞∞∞∞∞∞∞∞∞∞∞

BOOK TITLE: **CAUGHT IN THE ACT**
AUTHOR: Joan Lowery Nixon
PUBLISHER: Bantam Books, 1988 (Orphan Train Quartet)
FICTION
ISBN: 0-553-05443-0

READABILITY LEVEL: BOR: 3.5/ FLE: 5.0/ FOG: 5.0/ FRY: 3.0
DESCRIPTORS:
   Geographic Location: Missouri, near St. Joseph
   Dates: 1860
   Main Characters (race, sex, age, nationality)
      Mike Kelly (white, male, 11 yrs. old, Irish heritage)
      Hans and Irma Friedrich (white, approx. 40 yrs. old,
         German immigrants)
      Reuben Starkey (white, male, approx. 30 yrs. old, German
         heritage)

SYNOPSIS:
This book, the second in the "Orphan Train Quartet," concerns eleven-year-old Mike Kelly who is chosen by the Friedrich family to live with them on their Missouri farm. Mr. Friedrich is a dour man and a hard task-master, but Mike is determined to keep an open mind and do his best. This is difficult because fourteen-year-old Gunter Friedrich resents having a new "brother" and he conspires to get Mike into trouble whenever he can. However, all is not unpleasant for Mike in his new home. Mrs. Friedrich is a kind soul and an excellent cook, and Mike befriends Reuben Starkey and Marta, both of whom work for the Friedrichs. Mike works with Reuben every day, learning the

routine of farm work, including letting the cows out to pasture, chopping wood, and field work--all new skills for a New York City boy. Mr. Friedrich has a nasty temper and Mike, more than once, feels its painful effects. When Mike accidentally overhears snippets of hushed conversations between Mr. and Mrs. Friedrich, he is convinced that his new "father" is a murderer and Mike undergoes a number of adventures before the truth is finally revealed.

ILLUSTRATIONS: None

STRENGTHS OF BOOK:
Although based on true stories, this book is a fictional interpretation of what life might have been like for an orphan-train boy sent out West. While many pioneer families truly adopted these children as their own, there were others who took on the orphans as a means of cheap labor. This story is well-written, has plenty of action, and is hard to put down. It will appeal to both boys and girls and would make a good read-aloud selection for elementary school classes.

CONTENT FOR FURTHER DEVELOPMENT:
The story takes place in 1860 and the author mentions several historical events which might be further examined, including the slavery issue out West, Lincoln's impending election, and John Brown's activities in Missouri. Mike's unfortunate treatment at the hands of Mr. Friedrich might be discussed, including the ways in which Mike dealt with the problems he encountered.

∞∞∞∞∞∞∞∞∞∞∞∞∞∞

BOOK TITLE: **A FAMILY APART**
AUTHOR: Joan Lowery Nixon
PUBLISHER: Bantam Books, 1987 (Orphan Train Quartet)
FICTION
ISBN: 0-553-05432-5

READABILITY LEVEL: BOR: 6.2/ FLE: 7.5/ FOG: 9.4/ FRY: 8.0
DESCRIPTORS:
    Geographic Location: New York, NY to St. Joseph, MO
    Dates: 1860
    Main Characters (race, sex, age, nationality)
        Frances Mary Kelly (white, female, 13 yrs. old, Irish
            heritage)
        Mike Kelly (white, male, 11 yrs. old, Irish heritage)
        Various other members of the Kelly family

SYNOPSIS:
As this first installment of the "Orphan Train Quartet" opens,
two present-day children are visiting their grandmother in
Missouri and are bored as can be. In order to entertain them,
Grandmother reads to them the story of her great-grandmother's
life, who is Frances Mary in the story. The family history begins
in New York City in 1860 when Mrs. Kelly, a widow with six
children, is struggling to support her family. When eleven-year-
old Mike gets into trouble with the law, Mrs. Kelly decides to
send her children on one of the orphan trains leaving New York
for the West where she knows they will have a better life. The
Kelly children are devastated and it is up to the oldest, Frances
Mary, to keep the family together. She disguises herself as a boy,
Frankie, in order to remain with her youngest sibling, six-year-
old Petey. This story details the operation of the orphan trains,
including the long train journey, and takes the Kelly family to
St. Joseph, Missouri, where the six brothers and sisters are
parceled out to four different families. *A Family Apart* is
primarily Frances Mary's story as she adjusts not only to life
with a new family, but to life as a boy. The couple that chooses
Frances Mary and Petey are good, kind people, but Frances Mary
must come to grips with her mother's "betrayal" before she can
be at peace with herself and begin to create a new life in the
West. The reader is left with the promise of Mike's story in the
second book, *Caught in the Act* (1988). The third book is *In the
Face of Danger* (Bantam, 1988), and the fourth book, *A Place to
Belong* (Bantam, Feb. 1989).

ILLUSTRATIONS: None

STRENGTHS OF BOOK:
The author begins the story with a note regarding the history of the orphan trains operated by the Children's Aid Society between the years of 1854 and 1929. While not based on fact, this story was inspired by the true stories of these transplanted children, giving this book an air of authenticity. The story is well-written, with plenty of action, and it will appeal to readers of both sexes.

CONTENT FOR FURTHER DEVELOPMENT:
The political issues of 1860 are discussed, including Lincoln's election, the Fugitive Slave Law, and the underground railroad, and some of these will warrant further study. The whole topic of the orphan trains should be examined and the story's readers might consider how they would feel if they were suddenly taken from their familiar home environment and placed on a homestead in the West.

∞∞∞∞∞∞∞∞∞∞∞∞∞∞∞∞

BOOK TITLE: **ELIZA AND THE INDIAN WAR PONY**
AUTHOR: Paul and Beryl Scott
PUBLISHER: Lothrop, Lee & Shepard, 1961
FICTION
ISBN: None

READABILITY LEVEL: BOR: 5.5/ FLE: 6.0/ FOG: 7.8/ FRY: 6.0
DESCRIPTORS:
  Geographic Location: Kooskoosy River, Old Oregon Territory
  Dates: Approx. 1843-48
  Main Characters (race, sex, age, nationality)
    Eliza Spalding (white, female, approx. 7 yrs. old, American)
    Mother and Father Spalding (white, approx. 30s, American)
    Narcissa and Marcus Whitman (white, approx. 40s, American)

SYNOPSIS:
This book is based on the true story of Eliza Spalding, the first white child born in the corner of the Oregon Territory that is now the state of Idaho. The authors based their story on Eliza's book, *Memoirs of the West,* and on letters and diaries of people who lived in old Oregon. The Spaldings go to Oregon to be missionaries to the Nez Percé and Cayuse Indians. Eliza is born in the new country and grows up with the Nez Percé whose language she speaks fluently. Fearing she will not know the ways of her people, the Spaldings send Eliza to Mrs. Whitman's school at the Waiilatpu Mission on the Walla Walla. There Eliza meets more white children than she had ever seen before and learns deportment and how to read and write better. The Cayuse Indians are worried about the increasing numbers of whites coming over the Oregon Trail and fear for their lands. In November 1847, the Cayuse, never as friendly as the Nez Percé, massacre the white men and Mrs. Whitman at the Waiilatpu and take the remaining people hostage. Because of her fluency in Nez Percé, Eliza is unwillingly made to serve as a translator between the Indians and the hostages. Eventually the hostages are ransomed in late December and Eliza is reunited with her family.

ILLUSTRATIONS: None

STRENGTHS OF BOOK:
Many Native American customs are detailed in this well-written book and while there are hostile Indians, there are also many Indians who befriend the whites. Since this is based on a true story, the book is an excellent way to introduce history in a readable fashion. In the foreword the authors mention that one may visit Eliza's home in Spalding State Park and the Whitman National Monument, six miles west of Walla Walla, Washington.

CONTENT FOR FURTHER DEVELOPMENT:
One area for further discussion is the aim of the missionaries to "domesticate" Native Americans by instructing them how to plant crops and raise cattle rather than continue their semi-

nomadic way of life. The problem of land ownership was at the heart of the Whitman massacre and will need expansion. Also, were Eliza's parents justified in their fears that their daughter was turning out to be a wild heathen?

∞∞∞∞∞∞∞∞∞∞∞∞∞∞

BOOK TITLE: **THE PRICE OF FREE LAND**
AUTHOR: Treva Adams Strait
PUBLISHER: J. B. Lippincott , 1979
NON-FICTION
ISBN: 0-397-31836-7

READABILITY LEVEL: BOR: 4.7/ FLE: 6.0/ FOG: 6.0/ FRY: 6.0
DESCRIPTORS:
Geographic Location: Near Scottsbluff, NE
Dates: 1914-18
Main Characters (race, sex, age, nationality)
Merlin Adams (white, male, 31 yrs. old, American)
Edna Adams (white, female, 26 yrs. old, American)
Treva Adams (white, female, 5 yrs. old, American)

SYNOPSIS:
The recollections of Treva Adams Strait create the story of when her parents, siblings, and herself were homesteaders in Nebraska. The chapters cover the three-year period during which the Adams' were required to live on and work the land in order to procure its ownership. The reminiscences include such activities as wash-day, building the soddy, daily chores, school, and a tornado that swept through their land. Before the sod house was built, the family lived for a year in a tent which even survived the tornado. Merlin, Treva's father, rented out his land for grazing and was paid fifty cents for each animal that the local farmers sent to graze on his land. In addition, he earned money as an irrigation ditch rider and he grew potatoes, corn, feed grains, and watermelons on the homestead. The Adams family eventually received title to their land in July 1917. The afterword explains what happened to each member of the Adams family and to their hard-earned land.

ILLUSTRATIONS:
Reproductions of family photographs show the entire family, as well as the school, the tents, and the soddy. The use of the photographs lends a vivid historical sense to this autobiographical account.

STRENGTHS OF BOOK:
Aside from the first three chapters, which should be read or told together, each subsequent chapter could be read aloud separately to a younger classroom. The stories are told from a child's perspective which will appeal to younger readers and listeners.

CONTENT FOR FURTHER DEVELOPMENT:
The adult may need to explain why the chapters and recollections do not make this a story with a set plot. The children reading this book will need to remember that the author was only five years old when the story took place. It should be pointed out that even in the early decades of the twentieth century, people were still pioneering "out West" in much the same fashion as their ancestors had done more than half a century before.

∞∞∞∞∞∞∞∞∞∞∞∞∞

BOOK TITLE: **THE SODBUSTER VENTURE**
AUTHOR: Charlene Joy Talbot
PUBLISHER: Atheneum, 1982
FICTION
ISBN: 0-689-30893-0

READABILITY LEVEL: BOR: 4.9/ FLE: 6.0/ FOG: 7.2/ FRY: 5.0
DESCRIPTORS:
Geographic Location: Near Abilene, KS
Dates: 1870-71
Main Characters (race, sex, age, nationality)
Belle Warren (white, female, approx. 20s, American)
Maud McPherson (white, female, 13 yrs. old, American)
Quint Farwell (white, male, 16 yrs. old, American)

SYNOPSIS:
When Belle Warren arrives in Abilene after traveling from her Maine home to marry Silas Nelson, she discovers that he died the day before from consumption. His last wish was for Belle to take over his claim and she does exactly that with the help of young Maud McPherson who was nursing Silas. Primarily, this is the story of the efforts of these two women to make it on their own during the course of the fall, winter, and spring. In the late autumn they take in a "boarder"--a young cowboy named Quint Farwell who broke his leg during a cattle drive. The novel vividly depicts life on a homestead: the hard work, drudgery, poor food, and natural disasters, but also the rewards of seeing the fruits of one's labors. One memorable chapter deals with an invasion of grasshoppers that remained for two days and ate everything in sight, including the quilt that had been thrown over the well. Belle is a schoolteacher by profession and even though there are only nine children in the area needing instruction, she insists on conducting school in order to "civilize" the prairie.

ILLUSTRATIONS: None

STRENGTHS OF BOOK:
The book gives a realistic account of homesteading, yet does so in a readable and entertaining manner. It is noteworthy that a black family, the Martins, live on the prairie and Maud wonders if they were at one time slaves. The following quotation conveys the vast amount of space encompassing the plains: "Government surveyors had divided the whole state into sections, townships, and ranges. Everyone knew the number of the section where he lived. In a country without roads, hills, or even towns, there was no other way to describe your land." (p. 170.)

CONTENT FOR FURTHER DEVELOPMENT:
The role of women in the West merits further discussion. Conditions and circumstances in the West often forced women into "unfeminine" roles and behaviors, and Belle is an example par excellence. The numerous references to the outcomes of the

Civil War might indicate that people from both the North and South were moving west in an effort to rebuild lives shattered by the war.

∞∞∞∞∞∞∞∞∞∞∞∞∞∞

BOOK TITLE: **DAKOTA DUGOUT**
AUTHOR: Ann Turner
PUBLISHER: Macmillan, 1985
ILLUSTRATOR: Ronald Himler
FICTION
ISBN: 0-02-789700-1

READABILITY LEVEL: BOR: 5.6/ FLE: 6.0/ FOG: 8.8/ FRY: 6.0
DESCRIPTORS:
    Geographic Location: Dakota Territory
    Dates: Middle to late 1800s
    Main Characters (race, sex, age, nationality)
        Young woman (white, female, approx. early 20s, American)
        Matt (white, male, middle 20s, American)

SYNOPSIS:
A grandmother tells this story to her grandchild about what it was like to live in a sod dugout house on the Dakota prairie when she was first married. She describes how she first felt when she came into the sod house and how lonely it was with only the birds to talk to. She tells of the hardships of winter and of summer, and also of she and her husband's dreams for "dresses, buggy, some gold." Eventually the young couple are able to move into a clapboard house and the young woman is surprised to discover that she misses the warm, safe feeling of the dugout.

ILLUSTRATIONS:
Pencil sketches cover each page and depict the events in the story such as the earthy, close feeling of a dugout; the open, windy prairie; and the cutting and laying of the sod bricks.

STRENGTHS OF BOOK:
Great attention is given to the sounds and feelings of the prairie and of the dugout. The imagery may be too advanced for younger readers which makes this an excellent story to read aloud and discuss with the class. (NOTE: Although undoubtedly a picture book, the high readability levels are probably due to the long sentences in the book.)

CONTENT FOR FURTHER DEVELOPMENT:
The concept of a dugout house will need further explanation, as will other items mentioned in the book such as paper windows and silver boot hooks.

∞∞∞∞∞∞∞∞∞∞∞∞

BOOK TITLE: **THIRD GIRL FROM THE LEFT**
AUTHOR: Ann Turner
PUBLISHER: Macmillan Pub. Co. , 1986
FICTION
ISBN: 0-02-789510-6

READABILITY LEVEL: BOR: 5.9/ FLE: 7.5/ FOG: 9.0/ FRY: 8.0
DESCRIPTORS:
   Geographic Location: Dillman, MT
   Dates: 1885
   Main Characters (race, sex, age, nationality)
      Sarah Adam Goodhue (white, female, 18 yrs. old, American)
      Alex T. Proud (white, male, 60 yrs. old, American)
      Mr. Chang (Chinese, male, approx. 40 yrs. old)

SYNOPSIS:
Sarah is an eighteen-year-old woman living in Maine with no marriage prospects in her small town. She responds to an advertisement in the local paper asking for a woman to become the wife of a cattle rancher in Montana. As Sarah travels to Montana on the train, she encounters a fellow traveler who feels the Indians are ungrateful to the white men who, after all, have

provided "Car-rist-shun civilization" for them. Sarah is shocked when she sees how old her husband, Alex Proud, is, yet he seems to be as healthy as a much younger man. Sarah's first Montana winter is very cold and long, and Mr. Chang, the Chinese cook, provides Sarah with companionship while Alex and the three other hired hands are out on the ranch. Alex dies in an accident during the following spring round-up and Sarah is left with the entire ranch to manage. Bound and determined not to fail, Sarah decides to stay in Montana and operate the ranch.

ILLUSTRATIONS: None

STRENGTHS OF BOOK:
This book portrays the indomitable spirit of American pioneers who kept their bargains and worked against the odds to attain their goals. Sarah is a strong, independent woman, as many of the women on the prairie had to be, and although Alex wishes she would stay at home, Sarah insists on helping with the round-up. Her presence and efforts are appreciated by the ranch hands throughout the story.

CONTENT FOR FURTHER DEVELOPMENT:
By 1885 one could travel West on the railroad and students might want to compare the two modes of travel, steam engine versus covered wagon, including the length of the trips and the hardships entailed. The author makes numerous references to hygiene, such as having good or bad teeth, and this might be a topic worth pursuing. The whole question of mail-order brides should spark some discussion, especially how a teenaged girl today would react to having to marry a man more than three times her senior?

∞∞∞∞∞∞∞∞∞∞∞∞∞

BOOK TITLE: **BY THE SHORES OF SILVER LAKE**
AUTHOR: Laura Ingalls Wilder
PUBLISHER: Harper and Row, 1939
ILLUSTRATOR: Garth Williams

FICTION
ISBN: None

READABILITY LEVEL: BOR: 5.5/ FLE: 6.0/ FOG: 11.2/ FRY: 7.0
DESCRIPTORS:
Geographic Location: Dakota Territory, on Silver Lake, near
Brookins
Dates: 1879-80
Main Characters (race, sex, age, nationality)
Laura Ingalls (white, female, 12 yrs. old, American)
Mary Ingalls (white, female, 14 yrs. old, American)
Caroline and Charles Ingalls (white, approx. 40 yrs. old,
American)

SYNOPSIS:
Laura and her family leave their home in Minnesota and move
to a railroad camp in the Dakota Territory. Pa is the bookkeeper,
storekeeper, and timekeeper for the railroad company. Laura
loves the wildlife associated with Silver Lake and "sees
everything out-loud" for her sister, Mary, who became blind
after having scarlet fever. Laura is also fascinated with the
railroad construction and is delighted when Pa finally allows her
to observe the men working on the railroad. Ma is relieved
when the company moves on because she does not like her girls
growing up around such rugged men. Laura and her family
remain behind in the surveyor's house and spend the winter in
warm, spacious surroundings. When the spring rush for
homesteading begins, Laura and her mother spend day and
night providing food and a place to sleep for the men who have
come west to homestead. Soon a town arises where the railroad
camp once was. Eventually, the Ingalls family moves to the land
Pa claimed as their homestead which is a few miles outside of
town. It is here they plan to stay so that Laura, Mary, Carrie, and
Grace can get an education once a school is built.

ILLUSTRATIONS:
Pencil sketches at the beginning of the chapters visualize the
main idea for each chapter.

STRENGTHS OF BOOK:
The book realistically depicts the everyday life, both work and play, of a child old enough to have responsibilities. The railroad workers are portrayed as "rough" men, and, although the reader is not told any specific stories about them, it is conveyed that a railroad camp is not the ideal place for children. Even so, the author shows the better nature of these men when a French-Indian gambler and horse-thief comes to the aid of Laura and her family on several occasions.

CONTENT FOR FURTHER DEVELOPMENT:
The education of blind children in Laura and Mary's childhood could be compared with the mainstreaming practices of today.

∞∞∞∞∞∞∞∞∞∞∞∞∞

BOOK TITLE: **LITTLE HOUSE ON THE PRAIRIE**
AUTHOR: Laura Ingalls Wilder
PUBLISHER: Harper & Row, 1935
ILLUSTRATOR: Garth Williams
FICTION
ISBN: 0-06-440004-2

READABILITY LEVEL: BOR: 4.4/ FLE: 5.0/ FOG: 7.7/ FRY: 5.0
DESCRIPTORS:
    Geographic Location: Wisconsin to Oklahoma
    Dates: 1873-74
    Main Characters (race, sex, age, nationality)
        Laura Ingalls (white, female, 6 yrs. old, American)
        Mary Ingalls (white, female, 8 yrs. old, American)
        Caroline and Charles Ingalls (white, approx. 30s,
            American)

SYNOPSIS:
Laura and her family pack up their belongings in a covered wagon at the end of the winter and travel from Wisconsin through Minnesota, Iowa, Missouri, and Kansas, finally building a house in Oklahoma. The trip is long, arduous, and windy and they cross many rivers on their way. They chose their land and the site for their new home based on the water supply and the

animals they saw (e.g., wolves are a sign that deer are close.) Caroline helps to build the house until she becomes injured. Laura is excited about seeing Indians, but when they arrive at the house she is scared. The Indians come several times and take food, tobacco, and various other goods, but never harm anyone. The popular attitude was that if you did not hurt the Indians, they would not hurt you. When the family gets sick, a black doctor helps them to get well. Dr. Tan was a doctor with the Indians and had been passing by the house when he came to their aid. As part of the federal Indian relocation program, many Indians were forced to move their homes and a long procession of displaced Indians passes by the Ingalls home. At the end of the book the Ingalls are compelled to leave their homestead because they were three miles into the Indian Territory set up by the government.

ILLUSTRATIONS:
The illustrations by Garth Williams are done with a charcoal pencil and show much detail of the home, the prairie, and the Indians. Williams researched the route taken by the Ingalls for ten years before creating the pictures for this book as well as for all of the "Little House" books.

STRENGTHS OF BOOK:
All of the family's activities are told in great detail, especially how the house was built. Although the Ingalls liked and respected the Indians, one of their neighbors puts forth the opinion that the Indians did not belong there. Whether right or wrong, this view was held by many Americans of the time.

CONTENT FOR FURTHER DEVELOPMENT:
The question of Indian resettlement should be discussed. Has this situation been resolved today?

∞∞∞∞∞∞∞∞∞∞∞∞∞∞

BOOK TITLE: **LITTLE TOWN ON THE PRAIRIE**
AUTHOR: Laura Ingalls Wilder
PUBLISHER: Harper & Row, 1941

ILLUSTRATOR: Garth Williams
FICTION
ISBN: None

READABILITY LEVEL: BOR: 4.9/ FLE: 6.0/ FOG: 6.4/ FRY: 6.0
DESCRIPTORS:
Geographic Location: De Smet, SD
Dates: 1881-82
Main Characters (race, sex, age, nationality)
Laura Ingalls (white, female, 14 yrs. old, American)
Mary Ingalls (white, female, 16 yrs. old, American)
Caroline and Charles Ingalls (white, approx. 40s, American)

SYNOPSIS:
The long winter has passed and the Ingalls are back on their claim. Laura loves the spring weather and working outdoors while Ma and Mary take care of the indoor chores. However, when Pa tells Laura about a job sewing shirts in town, she cannot turn down a chance to earn some money towards sending Mary to college. Laura does not like working in town every day and hates being cooped up, but after six weeks she is able to contribute nine dollars to the college fund. Eventually there is sufficient money to send Mary to a college for the blind in Vinton, Iowa, and many hours are spent sewing dresses and preparing things for Mary's departure. Laura and her younger sister, Carrie, begin attending school in the fall and continue when they move to town for the winter months. Laura has a difficult time adjusting to the ways of the new schoolteacher, Miss Wilder, but she works at it. She attends her first sociable and is disappointed, but she greatly enjoys the literaries held at the schoolhouse every Friday night. Amidst all the gaiety, Laura has a hard time concentrating on her studies to become a teacher. She has wonderful times socializing with the "big girls and boys" in town, but realizes that over the summer she must study in order to pass the teacher exams. Even with the added distraction of Almanzo Wilder taking an interest in her, Laura is able to pass the examinations and becomes a teacher at the age of fifteen.

ILLUSTRATIONS:
Pictures of the town, literaries, and social events portray Laura's changing interests from being centered solely on her family and the prairie to including the importance of her friends and being fashionable.

STRENGTHS OF BOOK:
The story conveys a "family" feeling between all the townspeople and depicts in great detail the life in a small town-- a lifestyle not often written about in "pioneer" historical fiction.

CONTENT FOR FURTHER DEVELOPMENT:
Compare the community resources of Laura's town with the resources for children in the reader's community.

∞∞∞∞∞∞∞∞∞∞∞∞

BOOK TITLE: **THE LONG WINTER**
AUTHOR: Laura Ingalls Wilder
PUBLISHER: Harper & Row, 1940
ILLUSTRATOR: Garth Williams
FICTION
ISBN: None

READABILITY LEVEL: BOR: 6.2/ FLE: 7.5/ FOG: 12.8/ FRY: 8.0
DESCRIPTORS:
Geographic Location: De Smet, SD to Volga, Dakota Territory
Dates: 1880-81
Main Characters (race, sex, age, nationality)
Laura Ingalls (white, female, 13 yrs., old, American)
Mary Ingalls (white, female, approx. 15 yrs. old, American)
Caroline and Charles Ingalls (white, approx. 30s, American)

SYNOPSIS:
All the signs on the prairie indicate that the coming winter is going to be an unusually severe one. Consequently, Pa moves his family into the building in town that they rent out during the summer months. The snow begins in October and the

storms continue for three to four days at a time with normally one day of sunshine between blizzards. Carrie and Laura go to school when the weather permits, but when the school runs out of coal, it closes until the supply train can get to town. This does not happen, however, until early May and the families in town must get through the winter on whatever provisions they have. When the Ingalls run out of coal, Pa and Laura twist hay for fuel, and when they have no more flour, Carrie and Mary grind wheat grain in a coffee mill for their daily loaf of bread. Soon, that one loaf of bread is all the food they have to eat each day. Laura grows tired of the continuous sound of snow buffeting the building and of the darkness that prevails indoors when they run out of kerosene. Despite the many hardships, the family manages to keep their spirits up by reading aloud, working on their studies, reciting poems, and doing needlework. When the train finally arrives in the spring, the Ingalls have a wonderful Christmas dinner in May.

ILLUSTRATIONS:
Soft charcoal drawings portray such scenes as twisting hay, huddling around the stove for warmth, and sitting by windows for sufficient light to sew. The gauntness of the family's faces is even depicted when they are surviving only on brown bread.

STRENGTHS OF BOOK:
Through her writing, Laura Ingalls Wilder is able to relay the sounds, sights, and feelings connected with such a severe winter. The reader learns to what extent weather affects people, and the great lengths those people must go in order to battle the elements and survive.

CONTENT FOR FURTHER DEVELOPMENT:
Modern children are not often adversely affected by weather and they may have trouble comprehending the effect it had on the Ingalls and the rest of the townsfolk. When the family runs out of kerosene for light, Ma makes a "button lamp" by using some fat in a saucer for fuel, and a button covered with cloth as a wick. Readers may want to try this ingenious experiment under adult supervision.

∞∞∞∞∞∞∞∞∞∞∞∞∞∞

BOOK TITLE: **ON THE BANKS OF PLUM CREEK**
AUTHOR: Laura Ingalls Wilder
PUBLISHER: Harper & Row, 1937
ILLUSTRATOR: Garth Williams
FICTION
ISBN: None

READABILITY LEVEL: BOR: 4.6/ FLE: 5.0/ FOG: 5.0/ FRY: 5.0
DESCRIPTORS:
  Geographic Location: Plum Creek, Walnut Grove, MN
  Dates: 1874-75
  Main Characters (race, sex, age, nationality)
    Laura Ingalls (white, female, 7 yrs. old, American)
    Mary Ingalls (white, female, 9 yrs. old, American)
    Caroline and Charles Ingalls (white, approx. 30s,
      American)

SYNOPSIS:
This story picks up where *Little House on the Prairie* ends. The
Ingalls family has completed their journey from the Indian
Territory in Oklahoma and are now on the banks of Plum Creek
near Walnut Grove, Minnesota. They live for the first year in a
dugout cut into the side of a hill and the creek runs directly
outside their door. Laura milks her first cow and relishes the
prairie and the creek. When the first crop of wheat starts coming
up and looks as if it will be a successful one, Pa builds a house
with lumber, glass windows, and an iron stove. The family is
very happy about their good fortune. Laura and Mary attend the
school in town and meet Nellie and Willie Oleson. The family
attends church every Sunday and even makes a donation for the
church bell. However, when grasshoppers destroy the first
harvest, Laura and Mary must quit school to save their shoes for
the coming winter. Pa is forced to go east and earn money by
harvesting crops. After some time, he is able to earn sufficient
money to pay off part of the house and to buy some clothes for
his family. The Ingalls suffer more hardships when a blizzard
ruins the next crop, but they learn to overcome the bad times
and enjoy the challenge of their new life on the prairie.

ILLUSTRATIONS:
Charcoal drawings illustrate such hard tasks as fighting off grasshoppers and prairie fires, and finding one's way to the barn during a blizzard. Also shown with considerable detail is the use of a fish trap, the family's first Christmas tree, and jumping in straw stacks.

STRENGTHS OF BOOK:
The book depicts the many different kinds of hardships people living off the land had to face and how families overcame those difficulties.

CONTENT FOR FURTHER DEVELOPMENT:
The Ingalls are a very religious family and the book contains religious overtones. The role of religion in pioneer lives would be an interesting topic for further discussion.

∞∞∞∞∞∞∞∞∞∞∞∞

BOOK TITLE: **ON THE WAY HOME**
AUTHOR: Laura Ingalls Wilder
PUBLISHER: Harper & Row, 1962
NON-FICTION
ISBN: None

READABILITY LEVEL: BOR: 5.1/ FLE: 6.0/ FOG: 7.3/ FRY: 6.0
DESCRIPTORS:
   Geographic Location: De Smet, SD to Mansfield, MO
   Dates: 1894
   Main Characters (race, sex, age, nationality)
      Laura Ingalls Wilder (white, female, 27 yrs. old, American)
      Almanzo Wilder (white, male, 34 yrs. old, American)
      Rose Wilder (white, female, 7 yrs. old, American)

SYNOPSIS:
In 1894 the Wilder family leaves De Smet, South Dakota, where they have lived near Ma and Pa Ingalls, Mary, Carrie, and Grace, and begins their trip to Mansfield, Missouri, where they plan to

grow and harvest fruit.   An introduction by Rose Wilder explains life in her family and sets the story before the trek to Missouri begins.   The book, essentially a diary, is almost a day-by-day account of the trek from the day they depart De Smet until they reach their destination.   Laura describes the poor land conditions they see as they leave South Dakota, but which improve somewhat as they get closer to Missouri.   She also relates traveling conditions, weather, cooking, camping, and their surroundings.   Several of her entries contain descriptions of German and Russian settlements, including encounters with these immigrants and what their homes were like.   They meet many different kinds of people along the way, and many of the towns they pass through probably still exist today.   Footnotes by Rose give further explanation of some details and in the afterword she relates what transpired once the Wilders reached Mansfield and purchased their farm.

ILLUSTRATIONS:
The book contains many original photographs showing the family and their new home, cities, and bridges along their journey.   A map of their 650-mile trip is very detailed and follows the text closely.

STRENGTHS OF BOOK:
This book is the actual untouched diary of Laura Ingalls Wilder written during their trip in a five-cent Memorandum book.   The simply-written, easy to understand entries are valuable descriptions of the monotonous and long days associated with such a journey.   Also included are land and grain prices at that time.   The arrangement of the book makes it an excellent selection to read aloud to children.

CONTENT FOR FURTHER DEVELOPMENT:
Instead of moving west, the Wilder family traveled east in order to find a better existence.   What prompted this "reverse" action on their part?

oooooooooooooooooooo

BOOK TITLE: **THESE HAPPY GOLDEN YEARS**
AUTHOR: Laura Ingalls Wilder
PUBLISHER: Harper & Row, 1943
ILLUSTRATOR: Garth Williams
FICTION
ISBN: None

READABILITY LEVEL: BOR: 6.9/ FLE: 7.5/ FOG: 14+/ FRY: 8.0
DESCRIPTORS:
Geographic Location: De Smet, SD
Dates: 1883-85
Main Characters (race, sex, age, nationality)
Laura Ingalls (white, female, 16 yrs. old, American)
Almanzo Wilder (white, male, 23 yrs. old, American)
Various members of the Ingalls family

SYNOPSIS:
Laura teaches at a school in a claim shanty twelve miles from De Smet where she lives with the Brewster family. Mrs. Brewster is not at all happy about boarding the schoolteacher and makes sure Laura knows it. Laura tries her best to be as pleasant and helpful as possible and she barely manages to make it through the school week. Luckily, Almanzo arrives every weekend to take her away from the miserable Brewster home so that she can be with her own family. Teaching school is hard and many times Laura questions her capabilities, but by reminding herself that it will only last for eight weeks and that she must continue so that Mary can attend college, she is able to persevere. She is happy to return home and begin attending school again. Laura earns additional money by staying with a woman and her young daughter and helping them on their claim. When Laura gets her new teaching certificate she obtains a job teaching in a school near her home. She enjoys teaching in the new school and also spends a lot of time with Almanzo. Eventually he proposes, they are married, and move to Almanzo's claim, not far from town.

ILLUSTRATIONS:
The illustrations depict various places and activities throughout the book, such as the different school houses in which Laura teaches, the buggy and sleigh rides with Almanzo, and their marriage ceremony.

STRENGTHS OF BOOK:
Laura's experiences as a beginning teacher are historically supportable as typical of many young school teachers of the nineteenth and early twentieth century. Interview elementary teachers of today to find out how they were educated to become teachers.

CONTENT FOR FURTHER DEVELOPMENT:
The process of receiving and continuing teaching certificates may need further explanation. Laura must pass numerous exams each year and receives "third grade" or "second grade" certificates according to the results of those examinations. She also moves from school to school and teaches anywhere from two to four months at a time. Compare this to today's procedures in teacher education.

∞∞∞∞∞∞∞∞∞∞∞∞∞

Overland Journeys and Wagon Train Trips

GRADES K-3

BOOK TITLE: **THE JOSEFINA STORY QUILT**
AUTHOR: Eleanor Coerr
PUBLISHER: Harper & Row, 1986 (An I Can Read Book)
ILLUSTRATOR: Bruce Degen
FICTION
ISBN: 0-06-021348-5

READABILITY LEVEL: BOR: 3.4/ FLE: 5.0/ FOG: 4.6/ FRY: 2.0
DESCRIPTORS:
   Geographic Location: Traveling West to California
   Dates: 1850
   Main Characters (race, sex, age, nationality)
      Faith (white, female, approx. 7 yrs. old, American)
      Family members, including Mother, Father, and older
         brother

SYNOPSIS:
A young girl's family prepares to move to California in a wagon. Although there is not much room in the wagon, the girl manages to bring her pet hen, Josefina, on the journey. As the girl rides, she pieces together quilt squares describing various events of the crossing. The wagon train starts out with people in high spirits, but soon, hardships such as lack of food, deaths of people and animals, and having to leave items behind, are experienced and morale plummets. The pioneers trade with the Indians for food and water. Thieves come into the camp but are scared away by Josefina. Along the way Josefina dies and, once

the family's home is built, Faith and her mother piece together the quilt and it becomes her Josefina Story Quilt.

ILLUSTRATIONS:
The pictures by Bruce Degen follow the story line closely and Indians are shown with long braids, and some with a few feathers in their headbands.

STRENGTHS OF BOOK:
The lower reading level of this book is one of its best features and it describes in an understandable manner the hardships encountered by pioneers moving west. The Indians were not feared by the white settlers, rather, the Native Americans helped the people on the wagon train.

CONTENT FOR FURTHER DEVELOPMENT:
As the author explains, people in the West used quilts to document the history of their families and special events in their lives. An interesting discussion topic would be for children in the class to talk about how their families record experiences, for example, with cameras or videotapes.

∞∞∞∞∞∞∞∞∞∞∞∞

BOOK TITLE: **WAGON WHEELS**
AUTHOR: Barbara Brenner
PUBLISHER: Harper and Row, 1978 (An I Can Read Book)
ILLUSTRATOR: Don Bolognese
FICTION
ISBN: 0-06-020668-3

READABILITY LEVEL: BOR: 3.0/ FLE: 5.0/ FOG: 4.9/ FRY: 2.0
DESCRIPTORS:
    Geographic Location: Nicodemus, KS
    Dates: 1878
    Main Characters (race, sex, age, nationality)
        Johnny Muldie (black, male, 11 yrs. old, American)
        Willie Muldie (black, male, 8 yrs. old, American)

Little Brother Muldie (black, male, 3 yrs. old, American)
Ed Muldie (black, male, late 30s, American)

SYNOPSIS:
Shortly after the Civil War, Ed Muldie travels with his family from Kentucky to Nicodemus, Kansas. Their plan is to file for free land under the Homestead Act. Unfortunately, Mama dies during the journey. When the Muldies reach Nicodemus, a black settlement, they find an outpost consisting of dugouts instead of houses. The winter is very hard and the community runs out of food. They are saved from starvation by a group of Osage Indians who bring them food and fuel. In the spring, Ed Muldie leaves his boys to search for better land. The boys look after themselves for nearly four months and then, after receiving a letter and rough map from their father, they travel 150 miles on their own to be reunited with their father.

ILLUSTRATIONS:
The illustrations are done with colored leads, pens, and watercolors. The characters are drawn with brown pencil and are realistically depicted as Afro-Americans rather than dark Caucasians. The Indians are very sketchy but have apparent feathers and spears. The pictures on each page coincide with the narration.

STRENGTHS OF BOOK:
Wagon Wheels is a true story, based on the memoirs of Lulu Sadler Craig, a long-term resident of Nicodemus, and the author's note at the end of the book gives additional information. The story is intended for younger readers and it is simple, direct, and to the point.

CONTENT FOR FURTHER DEVELOPMENT:
The Muldie boys receive a letter and map from their father by way of a Post Rider. The readers may be interested in learning more about the postal system during the time the story takes place. It is not explained why Nicodemus, Kansas, was strictly a black community. It will be important to explain why so many black people, and whites as well, moved West shortly after the Civil War.

∞∞∞∞∞∞∞∞∞∞∞∞∞∞

BOOK TITLE: **THE WHITE STALLION**
AUTHOR: Elizabeth Shub
PUBLISHER: Greenwillow Books, 1982 (A Greenwillow Read-
    Alone Book)
ILLUSTRATOR: Rachel Isadora
FICTION
ISBN: 0-688-01210-8

READABILITY LEVEL: BOR: 4.1/ FLE: 1.0/ FOG: 5.8/ FRY: 4.0
DESCRIPTORS:
    Geographic Location: Texas, along the Guadaloupe River
    Dates: 1845
    Main Characters (race, sex, age, nationality)
        Gretchen (white, female, approx. 8 yrs. old, American)

SYNOPSIS:
This story is being told to a little girl named Gretchen by her
grandmother. It is the tale of the little girl's great-great
grandmother, also named Gretchen, who in 1845 was heading
West with her parents and three brothers and sisters on a small
wagon train. The author describes how the children traveled in
the cramped quarters of the Conestoga wagon and how hot and
airless it was. The four children are cranky and getting on each
others' nerves so Gretchen asks her father if she may ride their
old mare, Anna, for a while. Gretchen's father ties her to Anna
so she will not slip off and eventually Gretchen falls asleep in
the hot afternoon sun. At this time one of the wagons breaks an
axle and the train stops while it is being fixed. With the sleeping
Gretchen on her back, Anna wanders off following the trail of a
herd of wild mustangs and when Gretchen awakens she
discovers that she is lost. A white stallion mysteriously appears,
comes to Gretchen's aid, and the next day Anna leads Gretchen
safely back to the wagon train.

ILLUSTRATIONS:
The black-and-white drawings are simple, well-done and help convey the action in the story, including the uncomfortable conditions on a wagon train and the rugged western terrain.

STRENGTHS OF BOOK:
Although the book does not go into great detail about life on a wagon train, it does show the experience from a child's point of view. It will appeal to all children who love horses. This story is a good introduction to the westward movement for children just learning to read.

CONTENT FOR FURTHER DEVELOPMENT:
This book may lead into reading additional books about the trip west and settling in the West.

∞∞∞∞∞∞∞∞∞∞∞∞

BOOK TITLE: **GOING WEST**
AUTHOR: Martin Waddell
PUBLISHER: Harper & Row, 1983
ILLUSTRATOR: Philippe Dupasquier
FICTION
ISBN: 0-06-026332-6

READABILITY LEVEL: BOR: 2.5/ FLE: 4.0/ FOG: 3.2/ FRY: 2.0
DESCRIPTORS:
  Geographic Location: American West
  Dates: Middle 1800s
  Main Characters (race, sex, age, nationality)
    Kate (white, female, approx. 10 yrs. old, American)
    Family members, including Mother, Father, and older
      brother and sister
    Big Chokey (white, male, approx. 50s, American)

SYNOPSIS:
Kate narrates the story of her family's trip west. Besides her parents, Kate has an older brother and sister, Peter and Louisa. Pa gives Kate a diary to write her adventures in and this book's

narrative is written in diary form, with succinct entries. After Louisa and Mrs. Sullivan, a member of their wagon train, become ill after drinking contaminated water, Big Chokey stays behind with several afflicted families intending to catch up with the rest of the wagon train in a few days. The story is quite realistic--people die and the wagon train encounters both hostile and friendly Indians. As Big Chokey explains to Kate, the Indians were upset after the white men came and took their lands.

ILLUSTRATIONS:
The illustrations, an integral part of this picture book, are rich in detail and closely adhere to the text. They are almost done in comic-book fashion, with several scenes on each two-page spread. Colors are true to life and help depict the various hues of the prairie and mountains.

STRENGTHS OF BOOK:
The strength of this book is its realism and the fact that it is a picture book which can be read by younger students. Along this line it should be noted that the illustrations are quite graphic and do show wounded people falling down and people being hit by arrows. The book will appeal to readers of both sexes.

CONTENT FOR FURTHER DEVELOPMENT:
An area for further discussion might be the different reasons why some Indians were hostile to the white people while others were friendly.

∞∞∞∞∞∞∞∞∞∞∞∞∞

GRADES 4-9

BOOK TITLE: **WAGONS WEST: OFF TO OREGON**
AUTHOR: Catherine E. Chambers
PUBLISHER: Troll Associates, 1984 (Adventures in Frontier
        America Series)

ILLUSTRATOR: Dick Smolinski
FICTION
ISBN: 0-8167-0043-5

READABILITY LEVEL: BOR: 4.1/ FLE: 6.0/ FOG: 7.2/ FRY: 5.0
DESCRIPTORS:
    Geographic Location: Independence, MO, to Oregon
    Dates: 1854
    Main Characters (race, sex, age, nationality)
        Jed Stoddard (white, male, 14 yrs. old, American)
        Louisa Stoddard (white, female, 12 yrs. old, American)
        Jason Stoddard (white, male, early 20s, American)

SYNOPSIS:
When Jed and Louisa Stoddard are left orphaned in Virginia,
their older brother, Jason, who is now living in the Oregon
Territory, returns East by overland stagecoach to bring his
siblings out to Oregon where he has built a cabin and is about to
get married. Departing from Independence, Missouri, Jason
purchases the supplies they will need on the journey, and the
author details exact amounts such as 600 pounds of flour, 25
pounds of salt, and one bushel of dried beans. The wagon train
is lucky to have Jason since he is the only one to have ever made
the trip before, and he becomes the wagon master. This book is
really non-fiction in the guise of fiction because the story is full
of factual information designed to enlighten youngsters about
travel by wagon train before there were railroads and airplanes.
Besides harrowing experiences such as crossing rivers with
overloaded wagons, the story also relates mundane experiences
such as how the wagons traveled in four columns and how the
lead wagons moved to the rear of the train the following day so
that the same people would not always be riding in the dust
created by the wagons.

ILLUSTRATIONS:
There are simple black-and-white illustrations on each page
closely following the story line.

STRENGTHS OF BOOK:
This simply-told book is full of information about the logistics of wagon-train travel, including the supplies people had to take, how they traveled and lived each day, and even that the teams of oxen were all given the same names (Buck and Bright) so that anyone could drive a team.

CONTENT FOR FURTHER DEVELOPMENT:
The author mentions that the wagon train passed Court House Rock, Chimney Rock, and Independence Rock--landmarks which might warrant further exploring, especially since they can still be visited today. The author comments that "...the whole country had either Oregon Fever or California Fever." (p. 8.) The discussion leader may want to delve further into this historical phenomenon.

∞∞∞∞∞∞∞∞∞∞∞∞∞∞

BOOK TITLE: **DANNY**
AUTHOR: Lynne Gessner
PUBLISHER: Harvey House, 1979
ILLUSTRATOR: Donald Schlegel
FICTION
ISBN: 0-8178-5924-1

READABILITY LEVEL: BOR: 4.8/ FLE: 6.0/ FOG: 8.2/ FRY: 6.0
DESCRIPTORS:
Geographic Location: South Carolina to Salt Lake City, UT
Dates: Late 1850s
Main Characters (race, sex, age, nationality)
Danny Morrow (white, male, 16 yrs. old, American)
Claudia Morrow (white, female, 15 yrs. old, American)
Amelia and Herber Morrow (white, approx. 40 yrs. old, American)
Pico (Half-Navajo Indian, half-white, male, 20 yrs. old)

SYNOPSIS:
The Morrow family has decided to leave their home in South Carolina and resettle in Oregon. During the journey, however, the father, Herber, announces that instead they are going to Salt Lake City with a Mormon train. As they discover, not only has Herber converted to the Mormon religion, but he has even married a second wife. The family is distraught and they expel the father from their wagon, although they must continue with the wagon train or perish. Sixteen-year-old Danny and his younger sister, Claudia, are subsequently kidnapped by an Indian named Pico. Pico is a gentle man and he and Claudia fall in love. Despite this complication, Danny and Claudia leave Pico's village and make their way to Salt Lake City where they discover their father living in the streets, dying of alcoholism and consumption. After his death and burial, they return to their mother in Fort Laramie, Wyoming, and make plans to continue on to Oregon. Pico eventually returns for Claudia and decides to become a doctor in the white people's world.

ILLUSTRATIONS:
The black-and-white drawings correspond to the story's narrative.

STRENGTHS OF BOOK:
Many of Danny's preconceived ideas are shattered as he learns to overcome his prejudices against Native Americans and Mormons and begins to know them as individuals.

CONTENT FOR FURTHER DEVELOPMENT:
Because of their occurrences in the story, it may be necessary to explain some Mormon practices, such as polygamy, to children of non-Mormon faith. The conflict of cultures is personified in Pico, the son of a white man and an Indian woman, who speaks English and was raised a Christian. What difficulties did Pico experience in both the Indian and white worlds?

∞∞∞∞∞∞∞∞∞∞∞∞

BOOK TITLE: **TREASURE IN THE COVERED WAGON: A**
STORY OF THE OREGON TRAIL
AUTHOR: Vera Graham
PUBLISHER: J.B. Lippincott Co., 1952
ILLUSTRATOR: Howard Simon
FICTION
ISBN: None

READABILITY LEVEL: BOR: 3.8/ FLE: 6.0/ FOG: 6.0/ FRY: 2.0
DESCRIPTORS:
Geographic Location: Independence, MO, to Oregon
Dates: 1845-46
Main Characters (race, sex, age, nationality)
Flave-Ann Stone (white, female, 10 yrs. old, American)
Dan Stone (white, male, 13 yrs. old, American)
Belle Stone (white, female, 17 yrs. old, American)

SYNOPSIS:
This story is based on the author's great-grandfather who
emigrated from Missouri to Oregon in 1845--he is Dan in the
book. His sister, named Flave-Ann in the novel, insisted on
taking her melodeon (or organ, as she calls it) on the rugged
2,000-mile journey and she is the focus of the story. Flave-Ann
keeps a journal of the trip's events and this forms the basis of
the tale. Their wagon train contains about 60 to 70 wagons, half
of which will go to California and the other half to Oregon.
Flave-Ann occasionally plays her organ at the end of the day and
her music seems to lighten spirits and help people relax after a
long day's drive. The pioneers encounter trouble with the
Indians from time to time, the most notable incident being
when a small band of Pawnee Indians attacks the wagon train as
the travelers are having a dance. The author has a flair for
description and the reader will have a clear idea of how it was to
cross the Great Plains, including the heat, lack of water,
treacherous terrain, death, and disease, but also the incredible
feeling of accomplishment the travelers felt upon reaching their
destination.

ILLUSTRATIONS:
The simple black-and-white drawings help to visualize the grueling journey and they are scattered throughout the text. The inclusion of a map would have been helpful.

STRENGTHS OF BOOK:
The author apparently did considerable research and the book is historically accurate. One of the book's strongest points is that it relates that women and girls were just as helpful and important as the men were on the trip, sometimes driving the teams of oxen and herding the sheep.

CONTENT FOR FURTHER DEVELOPMENT:
Native Americans do not fare too well in this book. However, the settlers do meet several friendly groups of Indians along the way and they trade with the Indians at Fort Laramie. Flave-Ann views most of the Indians as filthy and one time as "stealing renegades," and this generalization will need further discussion.

∞∞∞∞∞∞∞∞∞∞∞∞∞

BOOK TITLE: **CASSIE'S JOURNEY: GOING WEST IN THE 1860s**
AUTHOR: Brett Harvey
PUBLISHER: Holiday House, 1988
ILLUSTRATOR: Deborah Kogan Ray
FICTION
ISBN: 0-8234-0684-9

READABILITY LEVEL: BOR: 5.4/ FLE: 6.0/ FOG: 10.4/ FRY: 7.0
DESCRIPTORS:
Geographic Location: Illinois to California
Dates: 1860s
Main Characters (race, sex, age, nationality)
Cassie (white, female, approx. 8 yrs. old American)
Plato (white, male, approx. 10 yrs. old, American)
Mama and Papa (white, approx. 30s, American)

SYNOPSIS:
Based on true accounts, such as those in *Women's Diaries of the Westward Journey* by Lillian Schlissel, the story of Cassie's family is presented in journal format. Beginning with deciding what and how to pack and saying goodbye to friends and family, the everyday events of the overland trail are told. Cassie describes children's jobs, the boredom, and routine events such as collecting buffalo chips, fixing supper, and rolling out bread dough that was gray with swarms of mosquitos. The landscape is described, particularly the well-known places such as the Platte River and Independence Rock where the wagon train celebrates the Fourth of July. While the hazards and sorrows of the trip are recounted, the feelings of shared accomplishments and mutual support among the pioneers ring true. A brief encounter with the Indians is for trading only. When the wagon train finally crosses the Sierra Nevada, Cassie and Papa spy the green valleys of California lying before them and rejoice that they are nearly at their new home.

ILLUSTRATIONS:
The soft black-and-white sketches convey a sense of place in the American West and the warm feelings among the characters. The team of Harvey and Ray successfully bring authentic text and portrayal of place together.

STRENGTHS:
This story is based on historical accounts of overland journeys to the Pacific. Harvey has included representative family experiences and conveys them through the fictional Cassie.

CONTENT FOR FURTHER DEVELOPMENT:
A discussion of the deaths of some of the wagon train travelers from sickness could lead to understanding the importance of medical technology and pure water for the pioneers and for today's children.

∞∞∞∞∞∞∞∞∞∞∞∞∞∞∞∞

BOOK TITLE: **FOR MA AND PA: ON THE OREGON TRAIL, 1844**
AUTHOR: Wilma Pitchford Hays
PUBLISHER: Coward, McCann & Geoghegan, Inc., 1972
ILLUSTRATOR: Peter Burchard
FICTION
ISBN: SBN GB 698-30425-X

READABILITY LEVEL: BOR: 4.0/ FLE: 4.3/ FOG: 5.5/ FRY: 4.0
DESCRIPTORS:
Geographic Location: Oregon Trail
Dates: 1844
Main Characters (race, sex, age, nationality)
John Sager (white, male, 13 yrs. old, American)
Louise Sager (white, female, 9 yrs. old, American)
Francise Sager (white, male, approx. 7-8 yrs. old,
American)
Four younger sisters, ages ranging from 3 months to 5 yrs.
old

SYNOPSIS:
As his parents remain deathly ill in the wagon with the new baby, John Sager wonders what will happen to his family on their journey to Oregon. When John is warned by Kit Carson that Indians are not far behind them on the trail, John is forced to move his parents, brother, and five younger sisters with the hopes of catching up with their wagon train which had gone ahead of them. Upon reaching the group, John discovers that his parents have died. After their burial along the trail, the Sager children continue on with the wagon train. The weary travelers eventually reach Fort Hall where they learn that the trail to Oregon is treacherous and practically impassable, so they opt instead to travel to California. However, John, wishing to honor his parents' wishes, resolves to continue on the Oregon trek. With the help of his siblings, Francise and Louise, John guides his family, two oxen, and a milking cow through deserts, Snake Canyon, and the Blue Mountains--all on foot. The children's feet become frostbitten, they are forced to leave the oxen behind, Louise breaks her leg, and the baby remains very sick, but eventually they reach the Whitman ranch in Oregon.

Young John Sager had successfully guided his family more than 700 miles, just as his parents had dreamed.

ILLUSTRATIONS:
The black, white, and gold drawings are rough looking and depict such scenes as gathering around the campfire waiting out a rainstorm and traveling in the snow. A map at the beginning shows the route taken by the Sager family. While the illustrations do not appear on every page, they are appropriately placed for transitional readers.

STRENGTHS OF BOOK:
The author wrote the story at a lower level and paced the action so as to be particularly suitable for younger readers. A note at the close of the book clearly explains the dispute between the United States and Great Britain over the Oregon Territory and hence why Americans were encouraged to settle there. Based on a true story, this book is about seven courageous children who played their part in claiming Oregon for the United States.

CONTENT FOR FURTHER DEVELOPMENT:
John Sager had to shoulder inordinate burdens following the death of his parents. Compare this to children's responsibilities today.

∞∞∞∞∞∞∞∞∞∞∞∞

BOOK TITLE: **TREE IN THE TRAIL**
AUTHOR: Holling Clancy Holling
PUBLISHER: Houghton Mifflin, 1942
ILLUSTRATOR: Holling Clancy Holling
FICTION
ISBN: None

READABILITY LEVEL: BOR: 6.1/ FLE: 7.5/ FOG: 9.7/ FRY: 8.0
DESCRIPTORS:
    Geographic Location: Santa Fe Trail in Kansas
    Dates: 1600-1840

SYNOPSIS:
The intent of this story is to depict how a Cottonwood Tree became a landmark along the Santa Fe Trail over a 200-year period. The story begins with an Indian boy and his uncle visiting the young Cottonwood. The boy piles rocks around the base of the tree to protect it from stampeding buffalo. The Indian tribe joins them and they camp there until buffalo are sighted and hunted. The boy hangs a buffalo tail in the trunk to thank the tree for bringing the tribe luck in the hunt. The tree then becomes a bearer of "messages": shot with the arrow of a Dakota Sioux in 1620; written on by a priest in 1623; pinned with the blade of a dagger by a soldier in 1631; and continually adorned with Native American trinkets. It becomes a legend, and when settlers pass by the tree they recognize it. Two frontiersmen, Jed and Buck, pass by often and one spring they notice that it has died. When they return later that spring they discover that the tree has been split during a tornado. Jed makes the wood from the tree into a yoke for his oxen and decorates it with the arrowheads and trinkets he finds in the trunk.

ILLUSTRATIONS:
Excellent, full-page, color illustrations detail the life, people, and events along the Trail. Diagrams of oxen yokes, wagons, and maps are also included as well as small, border drawings around the text. At the end of the book is a map of the region referred to in the book which includes the Native American tribes located in that region.

STRENGTHS OF BOOK:
This accurate and unusual tale is a succinct presentation of the events in the settlement of the West. It binds an Indian legend together with the American pioneers and other white peoples who crossed the Great Plains. It presents Native Americans as hunters and amiable people with a deep respect for the natural world.

CONTENT FOR FURTHER DEVELOPMENT:
The Cottonwood Tree is essentially the protagonist in this imaginative story and this literary concept may require some explanation.

∞∞∞∞∞∞∞∞∞∞∞∞

BOOK TITLE: **EDGE OF TWO WORLDS**
AUTHOR: Weyman Jones
PUBLISHER: Dial Press, 1968
ILLUSTRATOR: J.C. Kocsis
FICTION
ISBN: None

READABILITY LEVEL: BOR: 5.2/ FLE: 7.5/ FOG: 8.1/ FRY: 6.0
DESCRIPTORS:
    Geographic Location: Texas
    Dates: 1842
    Main Characters (race, sex, age, nationality)
        Calvin Harper (white, male, approx. 18 yrs. old, American)
        Sequoyah (Cherokee Indian, male, approx. 50 yrs. old)

SYNOPSIS:
This is the story of two unlikely traveling companions who are thrown together by an unfortunate turn of events. Calvin Harper is journeying on a wagon train heading East to attend law school. When a sudden Indian attack leaves Calvin the only survivor, he attempts to return to his Texas home. Alone on the desolate prairie, Calvin meets Sequoyah, an elderly Indian, who is also traversing the prairie by himself. At first Calvin distrusts the Indian, but when Sequoyah demonstrates that he is not violent like the Indians who attacked the wagon train, the two men agree to help each other survive on their lonely journey. Calvin is impressed that Sequoyah is engaged in writing a Cherokee alphabet and each one learns many lessons from the other.

ILLUSTRATIONS:
The black-and-white line drawings are realistic in their depiction of both the Native Americans and the whites, as well as of the stark terrain.

STRENGTHS OF BOOK:
Following a traumatic experience involving some hostile Indians, Calvin is able to change his perception of Native Americans based on his close relationship with Sequoyah. An Author's Note at the close of the book explains that Sequoyah was a real person, as was his walk halfway across the state of Texas.

CONTENT FOR FURTHER DEVELOPMENT:
The reasons behind Indian attacks on wagon trains should be discussed, including the graphic descriptions of the Indian massacre contained in the book. Was it unusual that Sequoyah was writing an alphabet of the Cherokee language? Did most Indian tribes have a written language? The concept of prejudice could be explored, and how one goes about changing people's perceptions and attitudes towards others.

∞∞∞∞∞∞∞∞∞∞∞∞∞∞

BOOK TITLE: **BEYOND THE DIVIDE**
AUTHOR: Kathryn Lasky
PUBLISHER: Macmillan, 1983
FICTION
ISBN: 0-02-751670-9

READABILITY LEVEL: BOR: 5.8/ FLE: 6.0/ FOG: 10.0/ FRY: 6.0
DESCRIPTORS:
Geographic Location: St. Joseph, MO, to California
Dates: 1849-50
Main Characters (race, sex, age, nationality)
Meribah Simon (white, female, 14 yrs. old, Amish)
Will Simon (white, male, approx. 40 yrs. old, Amish)
Various families on the wagon train

SYNOPSIS:
Shunned by his Amish community for a minor infraction, Will Simon decides to leave his family and head West to a new life. His adolescent daughter, Meribah, feeling stifled by the strict and inflexible Amish rules, forsakes her family to travel with her father. The Simons leave St. Joseph, Missouri, in April 1849 on a wagon train, and this book is Meribah's story of their trek across America. There are representative peoples on the wagon train that Meribah comes to know well--the Billings family from Philadelphia with their fine manners and china teacups, the Whitings, an elderly, childless couple, and the lower-class McSwats who are moving their entire family to California. Meribah's character is well-developed and the author skillfully handles her maturation and reconciliation of her Amish ways with those of the rest of the world. The author paints a lifelike portrait of what crossing America on a wagon train entailed. Her imagery is vivid and the reader can easily picture the changing prairie landscape and feel the heat and dust choking their lungs.

ILLUSTRATIONS:
Includes a map detailing the journey taken by the Simons.

STRENGTHS OF BOOK:
The book's major strength is its realism. It is also a moving tale of the human spirit and tenacity for life. The Indians are portrayed realistically and Meribah befriends several Indians along the way, including an Indian woman who teaches her about medicinal herbs and plants. The chapters are treated like diary entries, with dates and locations, and individual chapters may be read aloud. This book will especially appeal to female readers.

CONTENT FOR FURTHER DEVELOPMENT:
During the brutal trek on the wagon train, people underwent transformations in their attitudes, standards, and behavior. This psychological phenomenon may warrant further discussion. There is a rape in the book, very delicately handled, and this occurrence may or may not be further discussed.

∞∞∞∞∞∞∞∞∞∞∞∞

BOOK TITLE: **THE NO-RETURN TRAIL**
AUTHOR: Sonia Levitin
PUBLISHER: Harcourt Brace Jovanovich, 1978
FICTION
ISBN: 0-15-257545-6

READABILITY LEVEL: BOR: 6.4/ FLE: 7.5/ FOG: 12.0/ FRY: 8.0
DESCRIPTORS:
 Geographic Location: Sapling Grove, KY, to California
 Dates: 1841
 Main Characters (race, sex, age, nationality)
  Nancy Kelsey (white, female, 17 yrs. old, American)
  Ben Kelsey (white, male, approx. 18 yrs. old, American)

SYNOPSIS:
This novel is based on the true story of Nancy Kelsey, a participant in the Bidwell-Bartleson Expedition of 1841 traveling to California. This wagon train was the first to journey all the way from Missouri to California, and Nancy was among the first white women to make the trek. The wagon train contained about seventy people and they traveled along the Oregon Trail. Although most of the people had originally set out for California, many continued with their guide into the Oregon Territory. Nancy, her husband, Ben, their baby, and twenty-seven other pioneers continued on to California. The trail was rough and some of the settlers were forced to leave their wagons and many belongings along the way. Towards the end of their trip they kill the oxen for food, but finally arrive in California.

ILLUSTRATIONS: None

STRENGTHS OF BOOK:
The story is forcefully told and the reader will obtain a clear perception of the magnitude of the journey undertaken by these brave people. An epilogue explains what happened to each person from the train upon reaching California.

CONTENT FOR FURTHER DEVELOPMENT:
As the novelty of the journey wore off and the terrain and weather became more unbearable, tensions among the people manifested themselves. The trek often took six to eight months and children may want to consider how they would react under the same circumstances. Also, how would they feel about leaving their prized possessions behind and having to kill their oxen to survive?

∞∞∞∞∞∞∞∞∞∞∞

BOOK TITLE: **SAVE QUEEN OF SHEBA**
AUTHOR: Louise Moeri
PUBLISHER: E.P. Dutton, 1981
FICTION
ISBN: 0-525-33202-2

READABILITY LEVEL: BOR: 6.5/ FLE: 9.7/ FOG: 12.8/ FRY: 9.3
DESCRIPTORS:
    Geographic Location: Oregon Trail, near the North Platte
        River in Wyoming and Nebraska
    Dates: Middle 1800s
    Main Characters (race, sex, age, nationality)
        King David (white, male, 12 yrs. old, American)
        Queen of Sheba (white, female, 6 yrs. old, American)

SYNOPSIS:
King David and his sister, Queen of Sheba, survive a Sioux Indian raid of their wagon train along the Oregon Trail. Queen of Sheba has not been injured but King David has a large slash on his head where an Indian tried to scalp him. While many people lay dead around them, it does appear that others managed to escape. King David and Queen of Sheba set out to find them with only a single horse and minimal provisions. The going is rough and their progress slow due to King David's weakness, lack of food, and a very stubborn sister. After a while, the two children discover the tracks made by those who escaped, including their mother and father. After approximately one week they are met by a rescue party.

ILLUSTRATIONS:
A map of the area covered in the story would have been beneficial.

STRENGTHS OF BOOK:
In this book, two children resourcefully survive on their own and make very logical decisions.

CONTENT FOR FURTHER DEVELOPMENT:
While not indicative of the whole story, the description of the raid at the beginning of the book is quite gruesome. The reasons behind the Indian attack should be examined. The reader might notice the unusual first names of the two protagonists and speculate how they were chosen.

∞∞∞∞∞∞∞∞∞∞∞∞∞∞

BOOK TITLE: **SEVEN ALONE**
AUTHOR: Honoré Morrow
PUBLISHER: William Morrow, 1926 (Orig. pub. under the title of
        On to Oregon!)
FICTION
ISBN: None

READABILITY LEVEL: BOR: 6.7/ FLE: 7.5/ FOG: 9.9/ FRY: 8.0
DESCRIPTORS:
   Geographic Location: Oregon Trail
   Dates: 1844-45
   Main Characters (race, sex, age, nationality)
      John Sager (white, male, 13 yrs. old, American)
      Francis Sager (white, male, 11 yrs. old, American)
      Catherine Sager (white, female, 10 yrs. old, American)

SYNOPSIS:
The Sager family leaves their home in Missouri to travel to Oregon by way of the Oregon Trail. Thirteen-year-old John, who is a typical rebellious adolescent, runs away from the wagon train and meets misfortune with an Indian. Luckily he is rescued by Kit Carson who returns John to his family. After both

his parents die of disease along the trail, John becomes determined to continue the journey with his six younger brothers and sisters and to fulfill his father's dream.   They encounter many hardships on their trek, receiving occasional help from both whites and Indians along the way.   The author vividly pictures the grueling passage, including the sore feet and lack of shoes, chilblains, hunger, and the threadbare clothing that insufficiently protected them from the chill of winter. Eventually the Sager children complete their 1,000-mile journey to the Whitman Mission in Oregon.   The Sagers decide to remain with the Whitmans until John is old enough to file a land claim.

ILLUSTRATIONS: None

STRENGTHS OF BOOK:
The story is told from an adolescent boy's point of view and conveys his feelings as he takes on the overwhelming responsibilities associated with being the head of the family. This is based on a true narrative and is a remarkable adventure tale which will appeal to children of all ages.   This story was produced as a motion picture by Doty-Dayton Productions, and is also available as a video recording and filmstrip.

CONTENT FOR FURTHER DEVELOPMENT:
Numerous tragedies occur in the book, particularly the deaths of Mr. and Mrs. Sager, and these occurrences may need further discussion.   In addition, Mrs. Sager gives birth to a child along the way and the author does not provide much detail.   The Sager children encounter both friendly and hostile Indians, and the variant Native American attitudes towards the whites may be examined.

∞∞∞∞∞∞∞∞∞∞∞∞∞∞

BOOK TITLE: **WEST AGAINST THE WIND**
AUTHOR: Liza Ketchum Murrow
PUBLISHER: Holiday House, 1987

FICTION
ISBN: 0-8234-0668-7

READABILITY LEVEL: BOR: 5.1/ FLE: 5.0/ FOG: 6.8/ FRY: 5.0
DESCRIPTORS:
Geographic Location: Independence, MO, to Yuba River, CA
Dates: 1850
Main Characters (race, sex, age, nationality)
Abby Parker (white, female, 14-15 yrs. old, American)
Matthew Reed (white, male, approx. 18 yrs. old,
American)
Various members of the Parker and Reed families

SYNOPSIS:
As the story opens, fourteen-year-old Abby Parker, along with
her mother, older brother, Will, Uncle Joseph and Aunt Emma,
are preparing to depart Independence, Missouri, on their
journey to California. A year earlier, Abby's father caught "gold
fever" and he left for California, promising to send for his
family. It has been over six months since the family has heard
from him, and they are determined to find him. When
Matthew Reed appears on the scene, the Parkers take him on as a
hired hand to help drive the wagons. This book is the story of
this family's trek across the continent, how they began with the
highest hopes and how by the journey's end they had faced
tragedy and were near starvation. Mother has given Abby a
diary, which she calls her "river scrapbook," since she is noting
every river or stream they cross with the intention of later on
comparing her diary to the maps. Abby is a spirited girl who
hates doing "womanly jobs" and who would rather drive the
teams or care for the animals. There is some mystery behind
Matthew's appearance which unfolds as the story progresses, and
he and Abby develop a lasting relationship.

ILLUSTRATIONS:
The author included a clear, two-page map detailing all the
places along the Parker family's route to California.

STRENGTHS OF BOOK:
The story details some of the everyday things about the wagon train trip, such as the total lack of privacy, crowded conditions, and people's bad tempers, that are sometimes overlooked in children's literature. Throughout the book, Abby writes long letters to her sister in Ohio vividly describing the terrain and the events of their trip. The book is written in language for today's adolescents and will appeal to females, especially those who like romance and adventure.

CONTENT FOR FURTHER DEVELOPMENT:
Some of the characters underwent transformations throughout the six-month trek and as Mother says: "Sometimes I wonder if we've forgotten who we are, out here with only the wind for company." (p. 150.) The author mentions many things which could be discussed: The Truckee Pass to California and the Donner party; the Continental Divide; the odd Digger Indians in the desert; Chimney and Courthouse Rocks; and gold fever. The rigors of the trip brought about the early maturation of the teenagers in the story and this may merit some consideration.

∞∞∞∞∞∞∞∞∞∞∞∞∞∞

BOOK TITLE: **THE HALO WIND**
AUTHOR: Judith St. George
PUBLISHER: G.P. Putnam's Sons, 1978
FICTION
ISBN: 0-399-20651-5

READABILITY LEVEL: BOR: 4.3/ FLE: 5.0/ FOG: 6.5/ FRY: 5.0
DESCRIPTORS:
   Geographic Location: Illinois to Oregon
   Dates: 1845
   Main Characters (race, sex, age, nationality)
      Ella Jane Thatcher (white, female, 13 yrs. old, American)

Yvette Dumelle (half-Chinook Indian, half-French,
  female, 13 yrs. old)
Ma and Pa Thatcher (white, approx. 40s, American)

SYNOPSIS:
Ella Jane and her family have been traveling in a covered wagon
from Illinois since May 1845 and are now traversing the Oregon
Trail.   In August, Ella Jane's mother agrees to transport a
Chinook Indian girl named Yvette to the Dalles at the end of the
Oregon Trail so that she might be educated as a Christian. Ella
Jane's father decides to take the Meek Cutoff which is
presumably an easier and quicker route than the Oregon Trail.
Unfortunately, it does not prove to be so. The wagon train
encounters a very rough trail and eventually the travelers get
lost. Yvette, who does not wish to leave her tribe and who
resents the white settlers pouring into Oregon, also causes some
problems among the members of the Thatcher family. In the
end, Yvette returns to her family and the wagon train travelers
arrive at their intended destination.

ILLUSTRATIONS:
A map is included which illustrates the route taken by the
wagon train.

STRENGTHS OF BOOK:
This book is a realistic depiction of crossing the United States
from the Midwest to the Oregon Territory. An author's note at
the close of the book explains the background for the story and
what ultimately happened to the Chinook Indians.

CONTENT FOR FURTHER DEVELOPMENT:
The enormous tensions experienced by these people who had
been traveling together on the long journey might be explored.
Yvette was being sent to the white settlers in Oregon to be
"educated as a Christian." Why did her family wish to do this
and why did Yvette object? The bitterness of Yvette towards the
white pioneers is very strong and an important part of the plot.
Her feelings and actions could be used as the focal point of a
discussion on how the readers would feel in the same situation.

∞∞∞∞∞∞∞∞∞∞∞∞∞∞

BOOK TITLE: **TROUBLE FOR LUCY**
AUTHOR: Carla Stevens
PUBLISHER: Clarion Books, 1979
ILLUSTRATOR: Ronald Himler
FICTION
ISBN: 0-395-28971-8

READABILITY LEVEL: BOR: 4.3/ FLE: 5.0/ FOG: 5.2/ FRY: 5.0
DESCRIPTORS:
   Geographic Location: Independence, MO to Oregon
   Dates: 1843
   Main Characters (race, sex, age, nationality)
      Lucy Stewart (white, female, approx. 12 yrs. old,
         American)
      Will and Abigail Stewart (white, approx. 30s, American)
      Miles Chapin (white, male, approx. 12 yrs. old, American)

SYNOPSIS:
The author prefaces this story with an explanation of how the
Oregon Territory was claimed by both the United States and
Great Britain in the early 1840s and that many people emigrated
to Oregon in order to stake the claim for the United States. The
Stewart family leaves their Ohio farm and their wagon train
departs from Independence, Missouri, in May of 1843. Lucy's pet
Fox terrier puppy, Finn, is always getting into scrapes, scaring the
cattle and the chickens, and Lucy's father is constantly harping
on the dog. Lucy's mother is in the last stages of pregnancy and
Mr. Stewart is worried sick about her health. When Finn gets
separated from the wagon train Lucy runs back to fetch him and
gets caught in a sudden hail storm. She is found by a group of
young braves and although they can only communicate in sign
language, they take Lucy safely back to the train. The story is a
realistic depiction of westward travel and Lucy has daily chores
to complete such as helping her father unhitch the oxen and
checking for stones in the animals' hooves. There are also good
times in the book, including the game the children play every

night to see who can pick up the greatest number of buffalo chips--their primary source of fuel.

ILLUSTRATIONS:
The black-and-white illustrations are simple and while they portray characters more than the passing scenery, they still help to picture what the pioneers encountered on the crossing.

STRENGTHS OF BOOK:
This is a warm, human story of a family and their friends during a difficult journey that took six months. The author based some of the book on diaries, letters, and recollections written by actual pioneers and each chapter begins with a brief excerpt from one of these original sources. The Indians are portrayed favorably and in the afterword the author explains that it was not until the 1860s that the Indians became hostile as they witnessed the white people taking their best lands and killing off the great herds of buffalo.

∞∞∞∞∞∞∞∞∞∞∞∞

BOOK TITLE: **CAROLINA'S COURAGE**
AUTHOR: Elizabeth Yates
PUBLISHER: E.P. Dutton, 1964
ILLUSTRATOR: Nora S. Unwin
FICTION
ISBN: None

READABILITY LEVEL: BOR: 5.5/ FLE: 6.0/ FOG: 8.5/ FRY: 6.0
DESCRIPTORS:
    Geographic Location: New Hampshire to Nebraska
    Dates: Middle 1800s
    Main Characters (race, sex, age, nationality)
        Carolina Putnam (white, female, approx. 6-7 yrs. old,
            American)
        Mark Putnam (white, male, approx. 10 yrs. old, American)
        Annah and John Putnam (white, approx. 30s, American)

SYNOPSIS:
For over a year, John and Annah Putnam discuss the possibility
of leaving their rocky New Hampshire farm to homestead the
rich dark soil of Nebraska. As the family prepares to depart,
young Carolina is sad to be leaving the only home she has ever
known. After John buys a wagon, their "house on wheels," the
family encounters difficulty deciding what to take on their
journey. Carolina and her older brother, Mark, are permitted to
take only one treasure. Mark takes his valued compass, while
Carolina knows she will take her beloved doll, Lydia-Lou. The
Putnams leave New England in early May and, unlike many
other settlers who traveled west, they travel alone during their
four-month trip. Along the way the family sees remnants of
other settlers, including discarded rocking chairs, butter churns,
and even a ticking grandfather clock. In addition, they spy notes
left by other travelers, tucked under rocks, telling of nearby
watering holes and campsites. As they are near the Platte River,
Carolina befriends a Pawnee Indian girl, eventually exchanging
dolls with her. Although Carolina does not want to give up
Lydia-Lou, her father has taught her that pioneers must be
willing to share, especially with the Indians. Eventually,
Carolina's Indian doll is the family's safe conduct into the new
territory.

ILLUSTRATIONS:
The simple black-and-white illustrations follow the text closely
and are full of detail about the travelers and the terrain they
traversed. The pictures clearly evoke the family's love, warmth,
and concern for each other.

STRENGTHS OF BOOK:
This story is a realistic depiction of one family's journey west to
start a new life in Nebraska. The author relates considerable
factual information, such as the dimensions of the wagon, the
care of the animals, and everyday events during the journey,
and she presents it in a most readable and interesting manner.
Young children will understand the special relationship that

Carolina has with her doll, making this a good read-aloud selection for early elementary children.

CONTENT FOR FURTHER DEVELOPMENT:
Carolina's father understood the significance of being open and friendly with the Indians, but his attitude was not shared by many white settlers. The idea of prejudice might be a good topic to pursue with children. Also discuss Carolina's relationship with her young Indian friend; what would present-day children have done in Carolina's place?

∞∞∞∞∞∞∞∞∞∞∞∞∞

Immigration and the Immigrant Experience

GRADES K-3

BOOK TITLE: **WATCH THE STARS COME OUT**
AUTHOR: Riki Levinson
PUBLISHER: E.P. Dutton, 1985
ILLUSTRATOR: Diane Goode
FICTION
ISBN: 0-525-44205-7

READABILITY LEVEL: BOR: 3.1/ FLE: 4.0/ FOG: 4.0/ FRY: 2.0
DESCRIPTORS:
  Geographic Location: Europe to New York, NY
  Dates: Late 1800s
  Main Characters (race, sex, age, nationality)
    Sister (white, approx. 6 yrs. old, European immigrant)
    Brother (white, approx. 10 yrs. old, European immigrant)

SYNOPSIS:
As the story opens, a present-day little girl is hearing a story from
her grandmother about the girl's great-grandmother's journey to
America. Brother and Sister depart for the New World alone
since their parents and older sister have already traveled to
America. Their aunt sees them off with a barrel of dried fruit,
and asks an older woman to look after the two children.
Unfortunately, the woman dies on the trip, but Brother assures
his younger sister that he will take care of her. The traveling
conditions are poor and many people get sick, and after twenty-
three days, the weary travelers spy the Statue of Liberty. After
negotiating the Ellis Island maze, Brother and Sister are reunited
with their family. The children are delighted with New York

and with their top-story townhouse apartment which to them looks like a palace. Younger Sister is happy because now she can look out her window and see the stars come out.

ILLUSTRATIONS:
The soft watercolor drawings are beautifully done and depict the various portions of the passage from Europe to America, including the arrival in New York City. The illustrator captures the many emotions experienced by the immigrants, including their fears, discomfort, awe, and the joy of reaching their new country. Also, the warmth of the family's love shines through as the family is reunited.

STRENGTHS OF BOOK:
This story is a good introduction for young readers to the immigrant phenomenon in the United States. It is aimed for children and helps them to visualize what many of their ancestors went through in order to emigrate to a new land. The book is very suitable for reading aloud.

CONTENT FOR FURTHER DEVELOPMENT:
In this story, the two children traveled alone from Europe, leaving two younger brothers with their aunt, to be reunited with their parents who had earlier traveled to America. So, when Brother and Sister arrived in New York, they already had a settled home to go to. Many other immigrant families were not so fortunate and this may be a topic to pursue. In addition, many of the immigrants did not remain in the cities, but headed west to farm.

∞∞∞∞∞∞∞∞∞∞∞∞∞∞∞

BOOK TITLE: **PIE-BITER**
AUTHOR: Ruthanne Lum McCunn
PUBLISHER: Design Enterprises of San Francisco, 1983
ILLUSTRATOR: You-shan Tang
FICTION
ISBN: 0-932538-09-6

READABILITY LEVEL: BOR: 4.0/ FLE: 5.0/ FOG: 6.4/ FRY: 3.0
DESCRIPTORS:
  Geographic Location: American West
  Dates: 1865-85
  Main Characters (race, sex, age, nationality)
    Hoi (Chinese, male, approx. 16 yrs. old)
    Spanish Louie (white, male, approx. 40 yrs. old, Mexican)

SYNOPSIS:
This is the story about a young man named Hoi who comes from China in the 1860s to work on the transcontinental railroad linking the eastern and western United States. Hoi is still a growing boy when he arrives and is always hungry, so he begins to eat pies by the dozens--peach, apple, gooseberry, and carrot. His friends begin to call him Pie-Biter since he can eat pie and swing his axe at the same time. He becomes very strong and is called upon to help with some difficult situations that require his exceptional strength. Once the railroad was completed, some of the Chinese returned to their homeland while others remained in the United States. Pie-Biter decides to become a pack-train owner and he trains under Spanish Louie, all the while still baking and eating his pies. For fifteen years Hoi led pack trains and he became quite prosperous. But he missed his family and at the end of the book he decides to return to China to marry and have a family of his own.

ILLUSTRATIONS:
The Chinese illustrator skillfully blends Asian and western art styles, as evidenced in the following quotation from the book: "Though this book is predominantly western in tone, traditional Chinese techniques can be seen in the bold expressive strokes, fine line drawings, and decorative motifs." (p. [34])

STRENGTHS OF BOOK:
This enjoyable and humorous story instructs young children about the Chinese who came to America to build the railroads and how some of them settled in this country once their work was done. The Chinese were instrumental in railroad construction and hence are an important part of American western settlement.

CONTENT FOR FURTHER DEVELOPMENT:
The adult might want to explore the reasons why Chinese labor
was cheaper than American labor. In order to break into the
pack-train business, Pie-Biter deceives two Chinese pack-train
operators and the discussion leader may need to explain why
this type of deception might be warranted under certain
circumstances.

∞∞∞∞∞∞∞∞∞∞∞∞∞

BOOK TITLE: **THE LONG WAY TO A NEW LAND**
AUTHOR: Joan Sandin
PUBLISHER: Harper & Row, 1981 (An I Can Read History Book)
ILLUSTRATOR: Joan Sandin
FICTION
ISBN: 0-06-025194-8

READABILITY LEVEL: BOR: 3.7/ FLE: 1.0/ FOG: 4.6/ FRY: 4.0
DESCRIPTORS:
   Geographic Location: Sweden to New York, NY
   Dates: 1868-69
   Main Characters (race, sex, age, nationality)
      Carl Erik (white, male, approx. 8 yrs. old, Swedish
         immigrant)
      Mamma and Pappa (white, approx. 30s, Swedish
         immigrants)

SYNOPSIS:
Carl Erik's father is very worried. There has been no rain all
summer and without crops, his family will not have any food
for the winter. These are the "hunger years" of 1868 and 1869 in
Sweden and even the children are begging in the streets for food.
When a letter from Carl Erik's Uncle Axel arrives from
America, Pappa and Mamma decide to leave Sweden and join
their relations in the United States. Although a painful
resolution, the family sells their farm and belongings, packs
their trunk, and says good-bye to relatives and friends. From the
port of Gothenburg they travel by sea to Hull, England, and from
there they journey by railway to Liverpool. Here, along with

people from all parts of Europe, they board the steamship, *City of Baltimore,* for the uncomfortable, twelve-day crossing of the Atlantic Ocean. The story ends with the family's arrival in New York City where they find word from Uncle Axel welcoming them to their new home.

ILLUSTRATIONS:
The color drawings help convey the poor land situation in Sweden, the crowded traveling conditions, the fright and tension on the immigrants' faces, and the great sense of joy and hope upon reaching the shores of America.

STRENGTHS OF BOOK:
This is an excellent book to teach young readers about the immigrant experience in American history. Like thousands of immigrants, Carl Erik's family was drawn to America by good farm land, better job opportunities, and religious, social, and political freedom. Many of these industrious immigrants settled in the rich farmlands west of the Mississippi River and so contributed significantly to the development of the American West.

CONTENT FOR FURTHER DEVELOPMENT:
The diverse reasons that spurred European immigration to the United States in the second half of the nineteenth century should be discussed. This book will aid children in understanding the wretched traveling accommodations of the immigrants, especially during the Atlantic crossing when many of them became ill. The function of Ellis Island in the emigration process could be talked about, particularly since Ellis Island is currently being renovated as a national museum.

∞∞∞∞∞∞∞∞∞∞∞∞∞∞

GRADES 4 -9

BOOK TITLE: FRONTIER DREAM: LIFE ON THE
              GREAT PLAINS
AUTHOR: Catherine E. Chambers
PUBLISHER: Troll Associates, 1984 (Adventures in Frontier
              America Series)
ILLUSTRATOR: Dick Smolinski
FICTION
ISBN: 0-8167-0039-7

READABILITY LEVEL: BOR: 3.7/ FLE: 5.0/ FOG: 5.6/ FRY: 3.0
DESCRIPTORS:
    Geographic Location: Omaha, NE, and the Dakota Territory
    Dates: Approx. 1870-76
    Main Characters (race, sex, age, nationality)
        Katrin Isaacsen (white, female, 12 yrs. old, Norwegian
            immigrant)
        Nels Isaacsen (white, male, 8 yrs. old, Norwegian
            immigrant)
        Mama and Pa Isaacsen (white, approx. 30s, Norwegian
            immigrants)

SYNOPSIS:
Twelve-year-old Katrin is very distressed to learn that her father
has filed for land in the western plains of the Dakota Territory
which means abandoning their comfortable one-room cabin in
Omaha. Pa's family never owned land in Norway and the
Isaacsens emigrated to the United States in the hopes of
acquiring a farm. Their first summer in the Dakotas is spent
living in a tent and Katrin likes the flowering grasses, except for
the lack of trees and nearby houses. Mama and the children
travel by train to their new home which indicates the impact of
the railroad on the settlement of the West. The railway
companies advertised free lands in the West to Europeans and
this spurred a flood of immigrants. The Isaacsen family's move

to the Dakotas was part of the "Great Migration," although many settlers passed over the Great Plains because they thought crops could not be cultivated on land where few trees grew.   Once Katrin and her family arrive at their homestead, they must build a sod house and dig deeply for a well. The first winter the family returns to Omaha, but Pa remains to keep his claim on the land. The following spring the Isaacsens are reunited in their new Dakota home.

ILLUSTRATIONS:
The simple, black-and-white line drawings closely follow the text and are useful in picturing the events taking place. Included is a diagram of the new-fangled steel plow that was needed to cut the firm earth of the Plains.

STRENGTHS OF BOOK:
The book includes a fair amount of factual material that is well-integrated into the plot. The story shows how one immigrant family worked very hard in order to achieve their dream of owning a farm--something that had not been possible in their homeland. This story is available as a spoken recording.

CONTENT FOR FURTHER DEVELOPMENT:
There are many issues to generate discussion including the active role played by the railroads in recruiting pioneers; the impact of the Homestead Act of 1862; and how the lure and dream of the American West spurred so many Europeans to leave their homelands and how this contributed to the cultural diversity in the United States.

∞∞∞∞∞∞∞∞∞∞∞∞∞∞

BOOK TITLE: **THE IRON MOONHUNTER**
AUTHOR: Kathleen Chang
PUBLISHER: Children's Book Press, 1977
ILLUSTRATOR: Kathleen Chang
FICTION
ISBN: None

READABILITY LEVEL: BOG: 4.2/ FLE: 6.0/ FOG: 8.6/ FRY: 6.0
DESCRIPTORS:
   Geographic Location: Sierra Nevada Mountains
   Dates: 1866-67
   Main Characters (race, sex, age, nationality)
      Kwan Ming (Chinese, male, approx. 20s)
      Kwan Cheong (Chinese, male, approx. 20s)
      Kwan Hop (Chinese, male, approx. 20s)

SYNOPSIS:
Many Chinese men came to America to work on the Central-Pacific Railroad. They were not made to feel welcome in America, but still they worked very hard. Many died in accidents and fights while working on the railroad. The men who survived felt the need to help the spirits of their departed friends and brothers. They built a train, called the Iron Moonhunter, to seek out the spirits and provide them with a home. They used rails, parts of damaged trains, and mined gold and silver to create their ornate train in the shape of a dragon. The author includes an explanation of the legend at the end of the book.

ILLUSTRATIONS:
The illustrations are colorful and symbolic rather than realistic in style.

STRENGTHS OF BOOK:
The book discusses the problems faced by the Chinese railroad workers and how they may have used their own heritage and belief system to deal with those problems. This is a bilingual book whose text appears in both English and Chinese.

CONTENT FOR FURTHER DEVELOPMENT:
This book is somewhat on the mystical side and children may have difficulty distinguishing between fact and fiction. Students may benefit from learning more about the differences between the western and Chinese approaches to life and death.

∞∞∞∞∞∞∞∞∞∞∞∞∞∞

BOOK TITLE: RECOLLECTIONS OF A HANDCART PIONEER
  OF 1860: A WOMAN'S LIFE ON THE
  MORMON FRONTIER
AUTHOR: Mary Ann Hafen
PUBLISHER: University of Nebraska Press, 1983 (Orig. pub.:
  Privately printed, 1938)
NON-FICTION
ISBN: 0-8032-2325-0

READABILITY LEVEL: BOR: 5.2/ FLE: 4.2/ FOG: 9.9/ FRY: 6.3
DESCRIPTORS:
  Geographic Location: Switzerland to Utah and Nevada
  Dates: 1860-91
  Main Characters (race, sex, age, nationality)
    Mary Ann Hafen (white, female, approx. 6 yrs. old, Swiss
      immigrant)

SYNOPSIS:
The Stucki family, whose story is told in this book, emigrates to
the United States in 1860, crossing the plains with the last
handcart expedition to Salt Lake. The following year, the family
moves to St. George in southern Utah, and in 1891 they once
again relocate, this time to Nevada. Mary Ann Hafen begins the
recollections with the description of leaving home in
Switzerland, the Atlantic crossing, and the handcart trip across
the Great Plains. She includes remarkable details describing
their daily life, including both its pleasures and hardships. The
Mormon families worked together to develop farms, orchards,
cotton fields, and to expand the membership of the Mormon
church. While cooperative or communal life was tried, the
experiments did not last long. Polygamous marriages were
ordered by the church in order to allow more "persons in the
spirit world" to come to earth in human form. Difficulties in
the multiple-marriage families were common, but they
persevered with patience and industriousness. Mary Ann was
often left alone as her husband went on extended missions in
the United States and Europe, and while he was looking after his
other three families. Mary Ann's delight in her children, and in

the benefits of her hard work, are a large part of her story. Her Mormon faith was a constant in her life and aided her in accepting and surviving many hardships, and in recognizing the contributions of her family and church to the settlement of Utah.

ILLUSTRATIONS:
Included are many photographs of Mary Ann's family and their home.

STRENGTHS OF BOOK:
Among the book's strengths are its first-hand details of immigration, crossing the ocean, handcart travel from Nebraska to Utah, and life in the hot, dry southern Utah area known as "Dixieland." The influence of the Mormon church on lifestyle is described in a matter-of-fact manner. The courage and diligence of the Mormon pioneers is vividly documented in this recollection.

CONTENT FOR FURTHER DEVELOPMENT:
For non-Mormon children, the reasons for immigration and polygamous marriages will need explanation. In addition, Mary Ann Hafen's religious beliefs and faith may need further discussion.

∞∞∞∞∞∞∞∞∞∞∞∞

BOOK TITLE: **China Boy**
AUTHOR: Kay Haugaard
PUBLISHER: Abelard-Schuman, 1971
FICTION
ISBN: 0-200-71763-4

READABILITY LEVEL: BOR: 6.9/ FLE: 7.5/ FOG: 12.4/ FRY: 8.0
DESCRIPTORS:
    Geographic Location: Kwantung Province, China to
        California
    Dates: 1851-53

Main Characters (race, sex, age, nationality)
  Lee Sung Cheong (Chinese, male, approx. 18 yrs. old,
    Kwantung Province, China)
  Pan Chuan Hsi (Chinese, male, approx. 18 yrs. old,
    Canton, China)
  Hank (white, male, early 20s, Scandinavian heritage)

SYNOPSIS:
After his parents are killed and his home destroyed by a flood,
eighteen-year-old Lee Sung Cheong is left with a younger
brother to care for and a missing younger sister. Lee decides to
try his fortune in California where he can make money by
panning gold to send back to his brother. The labor recruiters
promise good pay and large homes and Lee also plans to use his
earnings to help search for his sister. Upon arriving in
California, Lee discovers that the attitudes of Americans towards
the Chinese are not positive or amiable. In short, the Americans
feel that the Chinese are taking all the available gold. Despite
these hostile feelings, Lee manages to make two good friends,
Hank and Pan, and the three men work together mining gold,
first in Hank's camp, and later on a claim Lee purchases. Lee
and Pan, another Chinese, encounter trouble with various
Americans who resent their being in California. However, Lee
succeeds in surmounting these difficulties and in saving
sufficient money to start a restaurant, as well as a new life in
America with his sister, Mei-Mei.

ILLUSTRATIONS: None

STRENGTHS OF BOOK:
The book addresses American sentiment and prejudices towards
the influx of Chinese immigrants and how the Chinese dealt
with these attitudes.

CONTENT FOR FURTHER DEVELOPMENT:
How did Lee hear about the Gold Rush in California so soon
after it happened? Why was China known as the Middle
Kingdom to the Chinese, while Americans just regarded it as
China? There are some rather stereotyped views of the Chinese

engaged in such activities as doing laundry and working as cooks. How are these stereotypes started and why?

∞∞∞∞∞∞∞∞∞∞∞∞∞

BOOK TITLE: **THE OBSTINATE LAND**
AUTHOR: Harold Keith
PUBLISHER: T.Y. Crowell Co., 1977
FICTION
ISBN: 0-690-01319-1

READABILITY LEVEL: BOR: 6.4/ FLE: 7.5/ FOG: 11.2/ FRY: 8.0
DESCRIPTORS:
Geographic Location: Cherokee Strip, OK
Dates: 1893-96
Main Characters (race, sex, age, nationality)
Fritz Romberg (white, male, 15 yrs. old, German heritage)
Fredric and Freda Romberg (white, approx. 30s, German heritage)
Various members of the Romberg family

SYNOPSIS:
The Romberg family leaves their home and family in Texas and travels to Oklahoma in order to participate in the land run of 1893. They have already chosen the land they want, but upon their arrival they find a family by the name of Cooper illegally settled there. The Rombergs are disappointed but not daunted, and they move to a less suitable adjacent plot. When Fredric, the father, suddenly dies, fifteen-year-old Fritz is left alone as the head of the family to battle the hostile ranchers, bad weather, and problem neighbors. By the end of the story, the Romberg farm is successful and the Rombergs manage to settle differences with their neighbors.

ILLUSTRATIONS: None

STRENGTHS OF BOOK:
The story is a realistic depiction of the troubles and hard work encountered by families who chose to farm in the Great Plains.

The author based the book on stories related by his two grandfathers who pioneered on the old Cherokee Strip, and on many other documented accounts of Oklahoma and Texas homesteaders. The book also delves into the reasons behind the strife between farmers and ranchers who were vying for the same land.

CONTENT FOR FURTHER DEVELOPMENT:
The phenomena of the extraordinary "land runs" of the late 1800s needs further discussion. The book does not mention how this land became available, i.e., that Native Americans were forced to relocate in order to make room for the white settlers. Mrs. Romberg was portrayed as a "typical" German wife who unquestionably obeyed her husband in all matters. What would an inquiry into the condition of women in the nineteenth century reveal about their legal rights?

∞∞∞∞∞∞∞∞∞∞∞∞

BOOK TITLE: **ELDER BROTHER**
AUTHOR: Evelyn Sibley Lampman
PUBLISHER: Doubleday & Co., 1951
ILLUSTRATOR: Richard Bennett
FICTION
ISBN: None

READABILITY LEVEL: BOR: 5.1/ FLE: 6.0/ FOG: 9.3/ FRY: 6.0
DESCRIPTORS:
    Geographic Location: Portland, OR
    Dates: Approx. 1920s-30s
    Main Characters (race, sex, age, nationality)
        Molly, or Ma-li (Chinese, female, 12 yrs. old)
        John, or Jeong (Chinese, male, 12 yrs. old)

SYNOPSIS:
The setting for this book is the Chinatown section of Portland. As the story opens, the Chan family has just adopted a twelve-year-old Chinese boy named Jeong. Molly, the main character in the book, encounters great difficulty in accepting her new brother, especially since he enjoys greater freedom than she does.

The four Chan daughters attend an American school during the day, but at night they spend four hours in a Chinese school. Jeong's adjustment to his new life is addressed, including the fact that he must learn English in order to go to school with his sisters. After some time elapses, Molly and Jeong accept each other and become fast friends. Together they organize a spy ring with the neighborhood children to help Chinese revolutionaries who are drilling in secret. The story ends with the birth of a baby boy, bringing the Chan family even closer together.

ILLUSTRATIONS:
The drawings depict the Chinese people dressed both in traditional Chinese costumes and American clothing.

STRENGTHS OF BOOK:
The author shows good insight into Chinese culture and customs. The Chinese are portrayed favorably both in their family relations and in their dealings with the American characters in the story. Religious tolerance is evident because although Mrs. Chan is a Buddhist, the children are allowed to attend a Christian church.

CONTENT FOR FURTHER DEVELOPMENT:
Explanation of such Chinese customs as men's braids and female footbinding will be necessary. Why did the Chinese children take on American names when they began at the American school? The activities of the revolutionaries will need to be explained, including the violence taking place. Was it plausible that a group of children actually acted as spies? The Chinese in this book did not treat the Japanese too well; was this a cultural phenomenon or a reflection of events occurring in the Orient?

∞∞∞∞∞∞∞∞∞∞∞∞∞

BOOK TITLE: **BETTER THAN A PRINCESS**
AUTHOR: Linda Lehmann
PUBLISHER: Thomas Nelson, Inc., 1978
FICTION
ISBN: 0-8407-6590-8

READABILITY LEVEL: BOR: 5.9/ FLE: 7.5/ FOG: 14+/ FRY: 8.0
DESCRIPTORS:
Geographic Location: Germany to Sedalia, MO
Dates: Late 1800s
Main Characters (race, sex, age, nationality)
Tilli (white, female, 7 yrs. old, German immigrant)
Albert (white, male, 10 yrs. old, German immigrant)
Melia (white, female, 5 yrs. old, German immigrant)

SYNOPSIS:
Tilli has been living with a family in Germany when she
receives word that her mother and father are in America and
have sent money for her to join them. Before her voyage across
the Atlantic even begins, Tilli discovers she has a younger sister
and older brother who have been living with other foster
families. Her young sister, Melia, speaks only Polish, but with
various kinds of signals, she and Tilli are able to communicate.
The journey across the ocean is very long, but the three "young
orphans" make many friends and are even given a cabin on the
second-class deck above steerage. Upon reaching America the
three children are distressed not to see their parents, but they are
helped by officers through the various checkpoints before
boarding a train for Missouri. Again they settle down for a
tedious trip. Tilli tries to imagine what her mother and father
must be like and she finds it hard to dispel the thought that her
mother is a princess. However, when the children eventually
reach their new home, Tilli finds that her mother is not a
princess, but something better--she is her very own mother.
Tilli's story continues in the sequel to this book, *Tilli's New
World*.

ILLUSTRATIONS: None

STRENGTHS OF BOOK:
The story is based upon the life of the author's grandmother and
depicts the tiresome journey immigrants had to make in order
to reach America. The three siblings utilize many different
forms of travel before reaching their destination and these could
be charted and then compared to forms of travel today. The

book is a valuable illustration of immigrant travel to the United States.

CONTENT FOR FURTHER DEVELOPMENT:
Because the story is based upon the recollections of an eighty-year-old woman, it is very sketchy in parts. A thorough explanation is not given as to why the parents left the children to go to America, although it is explained that the parents provided money to various officials to see that the children were well cared for. How common was this procedure? Upon reaching America, the children go through stations before being released. Since they dock in Baltimore, the reader cannot assume this is Ellis Island, but comparisons can be made. A follow-up discussion may include why most immigrants came to the United States and what they hoped to find here.

∞∞∞∞∞∞∞∞∞∞∞∞∞∞

BOOK TITLE: **TILLI'S NEW WORLD**
AUTHOR: Linda Lehmann
PUBLISHER: Elsevier/Nelson Books, 1981
FICTION
ISBN: 0-525-66748-2

READABILITY LEVEL: BOR: 5.1/ FLE: 5.0/ FOG: 5.4/ FRY: 5.0
DESCRIPTORS:
  Geographic Location: Missouri
  Dates: 1880s
  Main Characters (race, sex, age, nationality)
    Tilli (white, female, 8 yrs. old, German immigrant)
    Vina (white, female, late 30s, German immigrant)
    Anton (white, male, late 30s, German immigrant)

SYNOPSIS:
Tilli arrives in Missouri with her older brother and younger sister, where their parents have been preparing a home for them. Tilli is very excited about going to school but discovers that there is much work to be done on a farm and little time for schoolbooks. Tilli and her brother and sister eventually get to

attend school, but only sporadically and for short amounts of time. Two baby brothers die and the family is faced with hard times. In order to help support her family, Tilli works several times for and lives with other families, taking care of children, cleaning, and sewing. When she is home, Tilli is given much of the responsibility for taking care of her baby sister, Rose. When her mother, father, and brother leave to work on another farm for a few days, Tilli is in charge of both her younger sisters and saves Rose's life when she falls in the well.

ILLUSTRATIONS: None

STRENGTHS OF BOOK:
The story deals with the problems faced by immigrant families such as language barriers, feelings of prejudice from others, maintaining their heritage, and earning a living. Some German words, mainly numbers, are used in the story and their occurrence could provide a good opportunity to translate and learn numbers in another language.

CONTENT FOR FURTHER DEVELOPMENT:
Some questions, such as why Tilli and her siblings came to America after their parents, may be answered in the prequel to this book, *Better Than A Princess*.

∞∞∞∞∞∞∞∞∞∞∞∞

BOOK TITLE: **CARLOTA**
AUTHOR: Scott O'Dell
PUBLISHER: Houghton Mifflin, 1977
FICTION
ISBN: 0-395-25487-6

READABILITY LEVEL: BOR: 5.6/ FLE: 7.5/ FOG: 11.2/ FRY: 8.0
DESCRIPTORS:
  Geographic Location: California
  Dates: 1846
  Main Characters (race, sex, age, nationality)
    Carlota de Zubarán (white, female, 16 yrs. old, Spanish)

SYNOPSIS:
Patterned on the life of Luisa Montero, Carlota de Zubarán is an unconventional sixteen-year-old girl living with her grandmother and father during the time of hostilities between the Americans and the *Californios,* the Spaniards living in California.   The main conflict in Carlota's story is the Battle of San Pasqual, and Carlota is, in many ways, her father's substitute for her dead brother.   As an accomplished rider and horse manager, she accompanies her father to the actual battle fought against the gringos.   Afterwards, Carlota nurses her wounded father and an American soldier back to health.

ILLUSTRATIONS: None

STRENGTHS OF BOOK:
The details of the battle are drawn from the accounts and reminiscences of Juan Palomares, Christopher "Kit" Carson, and Lieutenant Emory, a topographical engineer with General Stephen Kearny's Army of the West--all actual participants in this engagement.   The historical context explores the place and contribution of the early Spanish settlers in California, as independent of Mexico, Spain, and the United States.

CONTENT FOR FURTHER DEVELOPMENT:
Carlota's character is far removed from traditional Spanish femininity.   While her strength and courage are admirable, readers may not recognize how unique her behavior is for the time and place.   The influence of Spanish culture in California and the American Southwest is an appropriate topic for further investigation.

∞∞∞∞∞∞∞∞∞∞∞∞∞∞

BOOK TITLE: **FIRST FARM IN THE VALLEY:**
                     ANNA'S STORY
AUTHOR: Anne Pellowski
PUBLISHER: Philomel Books, 1982
ILLUSTRATOR: Wendy Watson

FICTION
ISBN: 0-399-20887-9

READABILITY LEVEL: BOR: 5.6/ FLE: 6.0/ FOG: 8.0/ FRY: 6.0
DESCRIPTORS:
   Geographic Location: Latsch Valley, WI
   Dates: 1876
   Main Characters (race, sex, age, nationality)
       Anna Pellowski (white, female, 6 yrs. old, Polish heritage)
       Members of the Pellowski family

SYNOPSIS:
Anna's family and their Polish neighbors farm the land,
welcome new immigrants, and celebrate holidays with
traditional foods, songs, and games of Poland. Through the
events of the everyday life of the family, the motivation to
emigrate becomes evident. The Pellowski family experiences the
problem of being Polish and becoming American. The appeal of
the story lies in the ethnicity of the daily events of this
immigrant family who, with good humor and well-established
customs and values, become at home in their new country.
Children's jobs are well-depicted, with emphasis on the
importance and responsibilities of every member of the family.
The tragedy of deaths from diphtheria is dealt with in a realistic
and sympathetic manner. The characteristics of each family
member are appealingly defined. Based on the childhood
recollections of Anne Pellowski's great-aunt, *First Farm in the
Valley: Anna's Story* is the first of four books tracing four
generations of a Polish-American family. The other three books
are *Winding Valley Farm: Annie's Story* (Philomel, 1982);
Stairstep Farm: Anna Rose's Story (based on the author's own
childhood; Philomel, 1981); and *Willow Wind Farm: Betsy's
Story* (Philomel, 1981).

ILLUSTRATIONS:
Black-and-white drawings emphasize the Polish ethnicity of the
family and their neighbors with appropriate details and humor.

STRENGTHS OF BOOK:
The strength of the family ties, their values, and love for one another provide the setting for the immigrant story. Through the Pellowskis, the reader sees the process of becoming American while maintaining the ties and customs of their national origins. The glossary aids in understanding the Polish words that are used in the book.

CONTENT FOR FURTHER DEVELOPMENT:
References to Prussia and to Bismark may need to be clarified for the children. The importance of religion in the lives of the Polish immigrants adds to the realism of the book, but the customs may need further explanation.

∞∞∞∞∞∞∞∞∞∞∞∞

BOOK TITLE: **KIRSTEN LEARNS A LESSON: A
                SCHOOL STORY**
AUTHOR: Janet Beeler Shaw
PUBLISHER: Pleasant Company, 1986 (The American Girls
                Collection)
ILLUSTRATOR: Renée Graef; Vignettes by Paul Lackner
FICTION
ISBN: 0-937295-09-4

READABILITY LEVEL: BOR: 3.7/ FLE: 5.0/ FOG: 5.3/ FRY: 3.0
DESCRIPTORS:
    Geographic Location: Riverton, MN
    Dates: 1854
    Main Characters (race, sex, age, nationality)
        Kirsten Larson (white, female, 9 yrs. old, Swedish
            immigrant)
        Lisbeth (white, female, 11 yrs. old, Swedish immigrant)
        Singing Bird (Indian, female, approx. 9 yrs. old)

SYNOPSIS:
Kirsten Larson and her parents have been in the United States for four months, following their emigration from Sweden. It is

now November and Kirsten has just begun to attend the Powderkeg School, taught by the imposing Miss Winston. Still trying to learn the English language, Kirsten fears she will never fit into her new country, not to mention the school. When Miss Winston assigns each child to recite a poem in front of the class, Kirsten is terrified. Not only is she having trouble memorizing in a new language, but she is most afraid she will forget her poem and begin to cry in front of the whole class. One of Kirsten's delights in her new home is the little Indian girl she befriends by the river, Singing Bird. The girls communicate by hand signals and drawings and exchange little gifts. One day Singing Bird takes Kirsten to her small village where Kirsten meets more Indians and becomes familiar with Native American customs. When Singing Bird's village has to relocate because of poor hunting, Kirsten is saddened to lose her friend. However, Kirsten does take pleasure in successfully reciting her poem in school as she begins to finally "belong."

ILLUSTRATIONS:
The book contains soft color drawings which correlate with the text, helping transitional readers visualize the events. Archival photographs in the "Looking Back" section at the end of the story show authentic frontier schools, students, teachers, and school supplies.

STRENGTHS OF BOOK:
This story is an excellent depiction of a young immigrant girl's adjustment to life in a new country. Like all children, past and present, Kirsten has a child's normal anxieties at school--the frustrations and fear of failure, as well as the satisfaction of success. Without the prejudices of American white people, Kirsten makes fast friends with Singing Bird, although she has heard that Indians are "savages" and "cruel and bloodthirsty." A section entitled "School in 1854" at the close of the book details information about schooling at the time Kirsten's story takes place.

CONTENT FOR FURTHER DEVELOPMENT:
White peoples' negative attitudes towards Indians are touched upon in the story and may warrant more dialogue. Other topics

for discussion are the reasons why Native American hunting suffered once white settlers began to farm the prairies and why Indian villages had to constantly move. An excellent activity for children would be to compare prairie schools with their own school experiences by examining the physical layout, division of classes by age, school materials, and teacher education.

∞∞∞∞∞∞∞∞∞∞∞∞∞

BOOK TITLE: **MEET KIRSTEN: AN AMERICAN GIRL**
AUTHOR: Janet Beeler Shaw
PUBLISHER: Pleasant Company, 1986 (The American Girls
              Collection)
ILLUSTRATOR: Renée Graef; Vignettes by Paul Lackner
FICTION
ISBN: 0-937295-00-0

READABILITY LEVEL: BOR: 4.8/ FLE: 6.0/ FOG: 5.4/ FRY: 6.0
DESCRIPTORS:
  Geographic Location: Sweden to New York, NY, and
      Riverton, MN
  Dates: 1854
  Main Characters (race, sex, age, nationality)
      Kirsten Larson (white, female, 9 yrs. old, Swedish
          immigrant)
      Marta (white, female, approx. 9 yrs. old, Swedish
          immigrant)
      Various members of the Larson family

SYNOPSIS:
In 1854, Kirsten Larson's family is en route from their homeland in Sweden to start a new life in the United States. Kirsten's Uncle Olav has settled on a farm in Minnesota and the Larsons plan to join him there. On board their vessel, the *Eagle,* Kirsten meets a girl of her own age named Marta. By the end of their two-month passage, the two girls have become fast friends. Once they land in New York, Mr. Larson finds an agent who guides them on part of their overland journey to Minnesota. They travel by train as far as Chicago, where they meet up with Marta

and her family, and then they board a riverboat sailing up the Mississippi River. Unfortunately, cholera strikes the passengers and Marta succumbs to the illness. Kirsten is devastated, but she gets over the tragedy once her family is reunited with Uncle Olav and his wife and two daughters. Kirsten is delighted with her cousins, Anna and Lisbeth, and they quickly become friends and playmates as they explore the countryside. The Larsons have their own small log cabin and Kirsten truly feels she has now come home. Five other books by Janet Shaw follow this one in the American Girls Collection published by the Pleasant Company: *Kirsten Learns a Lesson: A School Story* (1986); *Kirsten's Surprise: A Christmas Story* (1986); *Happy Birthday, Kirsten!: A Springtime Story* (1987); *Kirsten Saves the Day: A Summer Story* (1988), and *Changes for Kirsten: A Winter Story* (1988).

ILLUSTRATIONS:
The soft color drawings enhance the text and help visualize what is taking place in the story. Vignettes at the close of the book depict what real immigrants may have looked like in the 1850s.

STRENGTHS OF BOOK:
The book details the immigrant experience of one Swedish family, but the events could easily be those of many of the European immigrants who came to America. A section at the end of the book entitled "Looking Back, 1854" explains why and how people came to America and what they encountered once they arrived, for example, the enormity of New York City, immigrant agents who cheated the foreigners who spoke no English, and finally, the rich farmlands of the Midwest.

CONTENT FOR FURTHER DEVELOPMENT:
The "Looking Back, 1854" section includes many details of the immigration process that could be examined, including how would a family decide what to bring and how did the passengers live and cook on board their ship during the Atlantic crossing. The immigrants' first impressions of their new country might be discussed, as well as the unscrupulous people who took advantage of these foreigners who did not know English.

∞∞∞∞∞∞∞∞∞∞∞∞∞∞

BOOK TITLE: **TO CALIFORNIA BY COVERED WAGON**
AUTHOR: George R. Stewart
PUBLISHER: Random House, 1954
ILLUSTRATOR: William Moyers
NON-FICTION
ISBN: None

READABILITY LEVEL: BOR: 4.6/ FLE: 5.0/ FOG: 7.0/ FRY: 5.0
DESCRIPTORS:
 Geographic Location: Council Bluffs, IA, to California
 Dates: 1844-45
 Main Characters (race, sex, age, nationality)
  Moses Schallenberger (white, male, 17 yrs. old, Swiss and
   German heritage)
  Elisha Stevens (white, male, approx. 40s, American)
  John Murphy (white, male, 17 yrs. old, American)

SYNOPSIS:
This is a true story based on the diary of Moses Schallenberger
who was in the "Stevens Party"--the first wagon train to cross all
the way to California. The party consisted of eleven wagons and
included twenty-seven men, eight women, and sixteen children.
The book details the many adventures, as well as the monotony,
of the trip West. The author is very informative and the reader
learns many things including how to make a covered wagon,
why oxen were chosen over horses to pull the wagons, and the
myriad of daily problems that beset the pioneers. The reader
shares the excitement of the travelers when they arrive at Fort
Laramie and can actually take baths, wash clothes, and eat proper
food. In addition, the author gives vivid descriptions of the
terrain and how it changed after crossing the Continental
Divide. The Stevens Party discovered what two years later
became known as the Donner Pass through the Sierra Nevada
Mountains and so opened up the road to California. At one
point Moses has to spend the winter alone in a cabin and his
survival story makes for exciting adventure reading.

ILLUSTRATIONS:
There are several maps that help the reader follow the trail made by the Stevens Party. In addition, there are many clear, three-color drawings throughout the text that help visualize how difficult the journey actually was.

STRENGTHS OF BOOK:
The author has done considerable research on the westward movement and is knowledgeable about such things as wagons, food, and the terrain. He writes very well and makes non-fiction read like fiction. This story is available as a spoken recording.

CONTENT FOR FURTHER DEVELOPMENT:
While Native Americans do not fare badly, the Digger Indians are portrayed as "almost like children" because when they visited the wagon train they took whatever items appealed to them. Did these Indians view their actions as wrongful? Other Indians, primarily in the person of the old Digger Chief, Truckee, were instrumental in enabling the Stevens party to reach their destination. What is the Continental Divide and why did the landscape change there?

∞∞∞∞∞∞∞∞∞∞∞∞∞∞∞∞∞∞

BOOK TITLE: **AN ORPHAN FOR NEBRASKA**
AUTHOR: Charlene Joy Talbot
PUBLISHER: Atheneum, 1979
FICTION
ISBN: 0-689-30698-9

READABILITY LEVEL: BOR: 5.7/ FLE: 7.5/ FOG: 9.0/ FRY: 8.0
DESCRIPTORS:
  Geographic Location: New York, NY, to Cottonwood City,
      NE
  Dates: 1872-74

Main Characters (race, sex, age, nationality)
  Kevin O'Rourke (white, male, 11 yrs. old, Irish
    immigrant)
  Euclid "Yuke" Smith (white, male, middle 20s, American)

SYNOPSIS:
After his father dies in Ireland and his mother on the ship to
America, Kevin O'Rourke arrives as an orphan in New York
City. Kevin discovers that his uncle is in jail, so he is left to fend
for himself. He sells newspapers on a street corner by day, and at
night he goes to the theater with the other newsboys. When the
boys are discovered sleeping in the lobby of the newspaper
building they are forced to sleep outside in doorways. When the
weather gets cold, Kevin and two friends decide to go to the
Newsboys' Lodging House, operated by the Children's Aid
Society. From here, children can become part of an "orphan
train" which sends children out West to be adopted by families.
Kevin joins a train with four boys and four girls on its way to
Cottonwood City, Nebraska. Kevin fears he will not be chosen
by anyone but ultimately he is selected by the editor of the
Cottonwood Clarion, the local newspaper. Kevin helps with the
printing of the paper, cooking, and goes to school. During the
winter, Kevin and Yuke live in a room behind the print shop,
but once the weather clears they move to Yuke's sod shanty on
his homestead claim. When Yuke's fiancée decides not to join
him in Nebraska, Kevin and Yuke decide to take time off from
the newspaper and visit Kevin's uncle, who is working on the
railroad.

ILLUSTRATIONS: None

STRENGTHS OF BOOK:
The book contains detailed accounts of how papers were put
together and published at the time and also depicts the lifestyle
and cooking habits of a nineteenth-century western bachelor.

CONTENT FOR FURTHER DEVELOPMENT:
The reader may want to do some research about orphan trains
and the role of the Children's Aid Society.

∞∞∞∞∞∞∞∞∞∞∞∞∞∞

BOOK TITLE: **SAMURAI OF GOLD HILL**
AUTHOR: Yoshiko Uchida
PUBLISHER: Charles Scribner's Sons, 1972
ILLUSTRATOR: Ati Forberg
FICTION
ISBN: SBN 684-12955-8

READABILITY LEVEL: BOR: 6.6/ FLE: 7.5/ FOG: 9.8/ FRY: 8.0
DESCRIPTORS:
Geographic Location: Wakamatsu, Japan to El Dorado
County, CA
Dates: 1869
Main Characters (race, sex, age, nationality)
Koichi (Japanese, male, 9 yrs. old)
Father (Japanese, male, approx. 30-40 yrs. old)

SYNOPSIS:
Following the death of their family, Koichi and his father leave
their homeland in Wakamatsu, Japan, and travel by boat with a
small group of people to California where they hope to begin
new lives for themselves. Their plan is to start a farm and raise
silkworms. Upon arriving in California they discover many
strong prejudices against them from some of the area residents
and bad luck befalls them. Despite adversities, they do find
friends in their neighbors, the storekeeper, and an Indian. They
even participate in a Native American ceremony honoring the
dead. Unfortunately, their attempts at farming fail and the
Japanese immigrants are forced to disband their Wakamatsu
colony and look for other employment.

ILLUSTRATIONS:
Ati Forberg's drawings are commendable in depicting Koichi's
attempts to adapt to a new life in America.

STRENGTHS OF BOOK:
A glossary in the back of the book aids in defining some of the
Japanese terms used and a detailed author's note helps to

determine the truth behind the story. The characters are well-developed and are portrayed favorably and justly. The conflict between homeland traditions and adjustments to a new country is clearly demonstrated.

CONTENT FOR FURTHER DEVELOPMENT:
The story contains several violent struggles which may need to be discussed. Koichi and his people face some rather blatant prejudices. Questions may be raised and need to be answered as to why such prejudices exist as well as the stereotypes which result from them.

∞∞∞∞∞∞∞∞∞∞∞∞∞∞

BOOK TITLE: **DRAGONWINGS**
AUTHOR: Laurence Yep
PUBLISHER: Harper and Row, 1975
FICTION
ISBN: 0-06-026737-2

READABILITY LEVEL: BOR: 5.3/ FLE: 6.7/ FOG: 7.5/ FRY: 6.3
DESCRIPTORS:
    Geographic Location: Chinatown, San Francisco, CA
    Dates: 1903-10
    Main Characters (race, sex, age, nationality)
        Moon Shadow (Chinese, male, approx. 8-15 yrs. old)
        Windrider (Chinese, male, approx. 30s)
        Relatives and members of the Company of the Peach
            Orchard Vow
        Miss Whitlaw (white, female approx. 40s, American)
        Robin (white, female, approx. 10 yrs., American)

SYNOPSIS:
Before eight-year-old Moon Shadow travels to America with his adult cousin, Hand Clap, he lived with his mother and grandmother in China where they looked forward to his father's letters and money from America. Moon Shadow learns to fly his father's magnificent kites, his only connection with his father. As the story is told from Moon Shadow's viewpoint, the

reader sees the shocking world of the *demons,* the Chinese term for white people, from the young boy's perspective. His father, Windrider, welcomes his son, as do the members of the Company of the Peach Orchard Vow, a Chinese laundry where the members, all male, live and work together. The father and son deliver laundry in the city and Shadow learns to ignore the insults and taunts from the *demons.* During a fight among Chinese men from different brotherhoods, Windrider kills a man in self-defense and to protect Shadow. They then move to another part of the city, where they live in the stable at Miss Whitlaw's home, and where Windrider does repair jobs of all kinds. Shadow's encounters with Miss Whitlaw and her niece start as fearful experiences, but over time, Miss Whitlaw, *a superior woman* according to the Chinese, and Robin become close friends and advocates of the Chinese immigrants. The San Francisco earthquake, recounted in chilling detail, forces white people and Chinese to flee the city. During the years of working for the laundry and in doing repair work, Windrider's dream is to build a biplane and fly as the Wright Brothers did. In correspondence with the Wrights, Windrider learns more about their flying machine. He and his son then move out of the city to build Dragonwings. The bond between the father and son, and their Chinese and white friends gives them courage to pursue Windrider's "dragoness."

ILLUSTRATIONS: None

STRENGTHS OF THE BOOK:
Seeing life in Chinatown in the early 1900s from the viewpoint of a Chinese boy reveals the fears and hopes of the young immigrant, as well as his inner strengths in facing the blatant prejudice against Asians. The varied personalities and characters are well developed so that the friendships and loyalty among the Chinese and with the Whitlaws illustrate the universality of such qualities. The friendship between Robin and Shadow is an important illustration of this theme. The depth of the characterization eliminates stereotypic portrayals of the Chinese and white people. The account of the earthquake is memorable.

CONTENT FOR FURTHER DEVELOPMENT:
Windrider recounts his long, complex dream of visiting the Dragon King, when he is given wings and flies. This dream sequence is important to the story, but some readers may need further explanation. Before Shadow learns to speak English, the *demons'* words are written in *italics*, which, for most readers is an interesting way of conveying that this is a foreign language to Shadow. The Asian Exclusion Act and its historical context will need further explanation. In the afterword, Laurence Yep cites a newspaper account of the twenty minute flight of Fung Joe Guey in 1909, as the catalyst for writing this fictional story.

∞∞∞∞∞∞∞∞∞∞∞∞∞∞∞

Native Americans

BOOK TITLE: **IN MY MOTHER'S HOUSE**
AUTHOR: Ann Nolan Clark
PUBLISHER: Viking Press, 1941
ILLUSTRATOR: Velino Herrara
NON-FICTION
ISBN: None

READABILITY LEVEL: BOR: 5.7/ FLE: 6.0/ FOG: 8.8/ FRY: 6.0
DESCRIPTORS:
Geographic Location: Tesque Pueblo, near Santa Fe, NM
Dates: 1930s-40s
Main Characters (race, sex, age, nationality)
Tewa Indian families of the Tesque Pueblo

SYNOPSIS:
Through teaching Tewa Indian children, the author records the children's view of their world. Through simple statements and descriptions the everyday life of the Pueblo comes alive. Via this approach, similar in vocabulary to an experience chart, the important aspects of Pueblo life are defined. The spiritual views of life are appropriately included, as in the following passage found on p. 24:
My heart is the holding-place,
My heart is the keeping place
For the things I know
About that lake in the mountains.
Always will I keep
In my heart

The things that belong there
As lakes
Keep water
For the people.

ILLUSTRATIONS:
The illustrations, some in color, portray Indian life both realistically and through Native American symbols. The drawings are essential to the story, particularly for younger children.

STRENGTHS OF BOOK:
The book's strength is in its concept development of the home life, people, environment, plants and animals of New Mexico as seen through the eyes of Indian children. This book is suitable for reading aloud to children.

CONTENT FOR FURTHER DEVELOPMENT:
Young children may need help in comprehending that much of the lifestyle portrayed is continuing today, but has been changed through technologies such as electricity, automobiles, television, and modern schools.

∞∞∞∞∞∞∞∞∞∞∞∞∞∞∞

BOOK TITLE: **I AM A PUEBLO INDIAN GIRL**
AUTHOR: E-Yeh-Shure' (Blue Corn)
PUBLISHER: William Morrow & Co., 1939
ILLUSTRATOR: Various Artists
FICTION
ISBN: None

READABILITY LEVEL: BOR: 4.3/ FLE: 5.0/ FOG: 5.6/ FRY: 5.0
DESCRIPTORS:
Geographic Location: Isleta Pueblo, NM
Dates: 1938

SYNOPSIS:
A Pueblo Indian girl tells of life in her Indian village. In short passages, she describes her country, home, the raising of corn, making bread, Indian clothing, and ponies. She also relates the importance of the earth to her people. Two especially poetic passages characterize beauty and birds.

ILLUSTRATIONS:
The illustrations were done by numerous Indian artists and full-page drawings accompany each passage. The defined lines and soft watercolors are pleasing to the eye.

STRENGTHS OF BOOK:
The book describes commonplace aspects of Indian life in simple language, yet touches upon the beauty of Indian poetry.

CONTENT FOR FURTHER DEVELOPMENT:
The story is somewhat out-dated and may lead to stereotyped views of Native Americans. It will be necessary for children to learn about Indian life today.

∞∞∞∞∞∞∞∞∞∞∞∞∞∞

GRADES 4-9

BOOK TITLE: **WAIT FOR ME, WATCH FOR ME, EULA BEE**
AUTHOR: Patricia Beatty
PUBLISHER: William Morrow & Co., 1978
FICTION
ISBN: 0-688-22151-3

READABILITY LEVEL: BOR: 7.4/ FLE: 7.5/ FOG: 13.6/ FRY: 10.3
DESCRIPTORS:
    Geographic Location: West Texas and New Mexico
    Dates: 1860s
    Main Characters (race, sex, age, nationality)
        Lewallen Collier (white, male, 13 yrs. old, American)

Eula Bee Collier (white, female, 3 yrs. old, American)
Mr. Cabral (white, male, approx. 40s, American)

SYNOPSIS:
Lewallen's father and older brother leave their farm in West Texas to fight in the Civil War. Shortly after their departure, the Collier family is attacked by a group of Comanche Indians and all but Lewallen and his young sister, Eula Bee, are killed. The brother and sister are taken, along with two siblings from a neighboring family, to the Comanche camp. The two small girls are accepted as members of families while Lewallen and Tom become slaves in different families. Lewallen learns how hard Indian women must work and soon gains the trust of his master, Many-Horses. When he is allowed to watch the ponies, Lewallen finds Fort Belknap and hopes the Confederate soldiers there will help him retrieve his sister. Unfortunately, there are too few soldiers and the risk is too high. However, Mr. Cabral, the father of two of the captives, is at the fort and he decides to accompany Lewallen to ransom Eula Bee. When Mr. Cabral is killed during a Yankee army raid on the camp where his son is being held, Lewallen is forced to find Mr. Cabral's family and ask their help in locating his sister. Lewallen eventually rescues Eula Bee from her Indian "family" and returns to Fort Belknap.

ILLUSTRATIONS: None

STRENGTHS OF BOOK:
While the book does portray the Comanche Indians as being ruthless in their raids on white settlers, it does balance the scale by describing a senseless raid by a white soldiers on an Indian camp. Indian captives are taken by the white men just as white captives are taken by the Indians. The story also portrays *Comancheros*, Mexicans in the Southwest who traded with the Indians, and the part they played in the conflict between Native Americans and white settlers.

CONTENT FOR FURTHER DEVELOPMENT:
Although the story focuses on the Indian raid, it should be stressed that raids by Indians on white settlements were on a

much smaller scale than those conducted by white people on Native American camps. Eula Bee's assimilation into the Comanche way of life might be discussed. Did she miss her own family? Why did the Comanches treat Lewallen and Tom differently than Eula Bee and Tom's sister? Compare Comanche customs to the customs of other tribes in Texas and the American Southwest.

∞∞∞∞∞∞∞∞∞∞∞

BOOK TITLE: **SUSETTE LA FLESCHE: VOICE OF THE OMAHA INDIANS**
AUTHOR: Margaret Crary
PUBLISHER: Hawthorn Books, Inc., 1973
NON-FICTION
ISBN: None

READABILITY LEVEL: BOR: 5.6/ FLE: 7.5/ FOG: 8.2/ FRY: 6.0
DESCRIPTORS:
   Geographic Location: Nebraska Plains
   Dates: 1854-92
   Main Characters (race, sex, age, nationality)
      Susette La Flesche (Omaha Indian, female, approx. 20s-40s)
      Francis La Flesche (Omaha Indian, male, approx. 20s-40s)
      Standing Bear (Omaha Indian, male, approx, 45-65 yrs. old)
      Thomas Tibbles (white, male, approx. 20s-40s, American)

SYNOPSIS:
This is a moving, tense account about Susette La Flesche, daughter of Chief Iron Eagle, who was educated at a mission school and later at an Eastern girls academy. After completing her education, Susette returns to the reservation to teach and becomes deeply involved in trying to promote Indian rights. She tours the United States with her brother Francis, Standing Bear, and Thomas Tibbles, her journalist husband. She addresses the issues of false treaties, inhumane confiscation of Indian lands, forced relocation of Indians, and the corruption of certain Indian agents. Susette, an effective, passionate activist for Indian land and voting rights, is unquestionably caught

between the old Indian lifestyle and adaptations to the dominant white culture.

ILLUSTRATIONS:
The book contains photographs of the major protagonists in the biography.

STRENGTHS OF BOOK:
This stirring account relates the Indian viewpoint of the conflict of cultures and identifies the pressures on the Indian crusader. Susette La Flesche is an authentic heroine.

CONTENT FOR FURTHER DEVELOPMENT:
Among some of the topics for further study are American manifest destiny, Indian relocation policies, the importance of tribal lands, and Indian voting rights. Were Indians granted their constitutional rights as citizens of the United States in the nineteenth century? In the twentieth century?

∞∞∞∞∞∞∞∞∞∞∞∞∞

BOOK TITLE: **A CIRCLE UNBROKEN**
AUTHOR: Sollace Hotze
PUBLISHER: Clarion Books, 1988
FICTION
ISBN: 0-89919-733-7

READABILITY LEVEL: BOR: 7.4/ FLE: 9.5/ FOG: 13.4/ FRY: 10.0
DESCRIPTORS:
  Geographic Location: St. Joseph, MO
  Dates: 1845
  Main Characters (race, sex, age, nationality)
    Rachel Porter, or Burning Sun (white, female,
      17 yrs. old, American)
    Leah Porter (white, female, approx. 16 yrs. old, American)
    Daniel Porter (white, male, 10 yrs. old, American)

SYNOPSIS:
Kata Wi, or Burning Sun, has been living happily for seven years with the Oglala Sioux since her abduction from a white people's fort by a group of renegade Indians. One morning, a party of white men come to Burning Sun's camp to reclaim her and take her back to be reunited with her family in Missouri. Kata Wi must now become Rachel Porter and resume life as a white girl--a life she barely remembers. Rachel's stern father forbids her to speak of her Indian life and family and burns all of Rachel's Indian clothing, thus destroying the last physical tie to her previous life. Rachel longs to return to her life as the daughter of the Sioux Chief, Waoka, and she encounters great difficulty in adjusting to life in the white world. Her young brother, Daniel, is curious about Rachel's Indian life and she delights in telling him Sioux stories. Rachel is quite concerned that she will forget Indian ways, so once she relearns how to read and write, she begins to write a series of notebooks detailing Sioux customs and folktales. Predictably, Rachel has to endure countless prejudicial attitudes and statements about Indians, for example, that Indians only engage in "stealing and killing." (p. 81.) One of Rachel's sources of happiness is being reunited with her Aunt Sarah who was also abducted at the same time as Rachel and who lived as an Indian captive of the Comanche. Aunt Sarah's death compels Rachel to resolve her own conflicting feelings about living her life as a white or a Sioux woman.

ILLUSTRATIONS: None

STRENGTHS OF BOOK:
This sensitive story is extremely well written and presents a viewpoint not often represented in children's literature--the return of an Indian captive who could not adjust to life in the white world. Rachel's life with the Sioux was very happy and she felt secure and content under the protection of her Indian family. Some of Rachel's writings are revealed in the novel, and through them, the reader comes to understand many Sioux customs and the Native American respect for and love of nature.

CONTENT FOR FURTHER DEVELOPMENT:
The conflict of Indian and white cultures will surely spur some discussion. It should be noted that not all Indian tribes treated their captives badly; indeed, in many instances white captives were taken into families as cherished daughters and sons. The white people's prejudices against the Indians might be explored, as well as the reasons why Rachel's father did not want her to speak of her Indian experiences. Daniel was very surprised to learn that the Indians did not have a written language and this phenomenon may be further investigated. Students might want to place themselves in Rachel's position and write their own ending to the story.

∞∞∞∞∞∞∞∞∞∞∞∞

BOOK TITLE: **THE MIDDLE FIVE: INDIAN SCHOOLBOYS OF THE OMAHA TRIBE**
AUTHOR: Francis La Flesche
PUBLISHER: University of Nebraska Press, 1978 (Orig. pub.: Small, Maynard, 1900)
NON-FICTION
ISBN: 0-8032-2852-X

READABILITY LEVEL: BOR: 6.1/ FLE: 12.0/ FOG: 14+/ FRY: 10.0
DESCRIPTORS:
    Geographic Location: Nebraska
    Dates: Middle 1860s
    Main Characters (race, sex, age, nationality)
    Five Omaha Indian boys of elementary-school age

SYNOPSIS:
This a high-spirited account of friendship among a group of Omaha Indian schoolboys attending the Presbyterian Mission School near Omaha City in the 1860s. Their pranks, games, loyalty, and learning take place between two cultures, Omaha Indian and white. While the missionaries try to make them into "make-believe white men," the Indian boys cling to many of their family and tribal traditions. While the boys are

forbidden to speak anything but English, they develop their own communication system and loyalties, despite Gray-Beard, their teacher. Beneath the childish good times and humorous events lie the hardships and heartaches of being away from home and forced into a new way of life. The boyish behavior rings true, as does the compassion among the Middle Five.

ILLUSTRATIONS:
Included are a few photographs of the Mission School.

STRENGTHS OF BOOK:
The boys' behavior and conversations are realistic and full of fun, while the setting, both time and place, emphasize the problems of this transitional period in the history of Native Americans.

CONTENT FOR FURTHER DEVELOPMENT:
As with any stories of Indian life, the time and place must be stressed with children so as to have an appropriate historical perspective for the setting and events. The role of the missionaries in the education of Indian children must have some background discussion. Information about current educational practices should also be examined.

∞∞∞∞∞∞∞∞∞∞∞∞

BOOK TITLE: **SQUAW MAN'S SON**
AUTHOR: Evelyn Sibley Lampman
PUBLISHER: Atheneum, 1978
ILLUSTRATOR: Map by Anita Karl
FICTION
ISBN: 0-689-50102-1

READABILITY LEVEL: BOR: 6.5/ FLE: 9.5/ FOG: 14+/ FRY: 8.0
DESCRIPTORS:
　　Geographic Location: Border between California and Oregon,
　　　　Lower Klamath Lake and Tule Lake, Linkville, OR
　　Dates: 1873
　　Main Characters (race, sex, age, nationality)
　　　　Billy Morrison (half-Modoc Indian, half-white, male,

13 yrs. old)
Mose Morrison (white, male, approx. 40 yrs. old,
   American)
Captain Jack (Modoc Indian, male, approx. 30s)

SYNOPSIS:
Billy lives in Linkville, Oregon, with his white father and Indian mother. Billy and his father, Mose, are looked down upon by the townspeople because of their association with Billy's mother and Mose is known as "Squaw Man." Billy's father is offered a position as a deputy sheriff, but he can only accept the job if his wife leaves. She departs to live with her tribe in California and eventually Billy follows, where he is readily accepted by the Indians. When the white soldiers tell the tribe that they must once again move to another reservation, they decide to stand their ground. Although the Chief, named Captain Jack, prefers to do things quietly, the majority of the tribe wishes to fight, and they do so. In the ensuing battle, many white lives are lost although the Indians suffer few casualties. Ultimately, Captain Jack and five other Indians are tried for murder. Four of the Indians were executed and two received life imprisonment. The Indians and the United States army officers in the book are real, as is their story. Billy, his family, and the town are fictitious.

ILLUSTRATIONS:
The book includes a map of the area, although it is a little unclear.

STRENGTHS OF BOOK:
The factual basis of the book is one of its strong points. It realistically shows that sometimes conflict occurred within Indian tribes when some preferred to fight and others did not. The Modoc Indians had already moved once, peacefully, and the Indians did not feel they should have to move again. This story will probably appeal more to boys than to girls.

CONTENT FOR FURTHER DEVELOPMENT:
The whole question of Indian resettlement might be explored further. Why did the Army have the authority to force the

Indians to move? Was it fair that the Modocs had to uproot themselves twice in a short span of time? What kind of land were they given? Students might want to compare the map included in the book with a current atlas to see what has changed.

∞∞∞∞∞∞∞∞∞∞∞∞∞∞

BOOK TITLE: **WHITE CAPTIVES**
AUTHOR: Evelyn Sibley Lampman
PUBLISHER: Atheneum, 1975
FICTION
ISBN: 0-689-50023-8

READABILITY LEVEL: BOR: 5.5/ FLE: 6.0/ FOG: 8.5/ FRY: 6.0
DESCRIPTORS:
Geographic Location: Rio Grande Area, NM
Dates: 1851-56
Main Characters (race, sex, age, nationality)
Olive Oatman (white, female, 12 yrs. old, Mormon)
Mary Ann Oatman (white, female, 7 yrs. old, Mormon)
Topeka (Mohave Indian, female, approx. 13 yrs. old)
Vimaka (Mohave Indian, female, approx. 40 yrs. old)

SYNOPSIS:
In 1850 the Oatman family leaves their farm in Illinois and heads for New Mexico with a small group of fifty people to start a new Mormon settlement. In March of 1851 the Oatman wagon, with two adults and seven children, goes on alone and is attacked by a band of Tonto Apaches. All are killed except for fifteen-year-old Lorenzo, and two sisters, Olive and Mary Ann, who are taken captive. The girls are enslaved in retaliation for two Indian women who had been taken by white raiders and this novel relates the lives of the Oatman sisters in captivity. They stay with the Tontos for a year and then are sold as slaves to the Mohave Indians. While with the Tontos their lives are hard, but the Indians do not treat them cruelly. Olive and Mary Ann fare somewhat better with the Mohave Indians as the house slaves of the Chief, Espaniol. The Chief's daughter, Topeka, trains them and eventually the Oatman girls become

like family to this Indian household. The girls work hard, carrying water, wood, and digging roots, but no harder than most Indian women.

ILLUSTRATIONS: None

STRENGTHS OF BOOK:
The book is based on a true story and thus is valuable from a historical perspective. One of the book's major strengths is its depiction of life in a Native American village, in this case, of the Mohave Indians. Their customs and attitudes are revealed and it is noteworthy that they did not mistreat their white captives. Indeed, the Indians learned a few things from the girls and were quite entranced by their hymn singing.

CONTENT FOR FURTHER DEVELOPMENT:
The complex Indian-white relationship needs additional study. The author's note at the close of the book relates what happened after Olive Oatman was rescued and her subsequent lecturing and written account of her ordeal. As the years went by, Olive's view of the Indians became darker and this occurrence may need further discussion.

∞∞∞∞∞∞∞∞∞∞∞∞∞

BOOK TITLE: **PRETTY-SHIELD: MEDICINE WOMAN OF THE CROWS**
AUTHOR: Frank B. Linderman
PUBLISHER: University of Nebraska Press, 1974 (Orig. pub.
under the title *Red Mother*. John Day Co., 1932)
NON-FICTION
ISBN: 0-8032-5791-0

READABILITY LEVEL: BOR: 5.4/ FLE: 7.5/ FOG: 11.6/ FRY: 8.0
DESCRIPTORS:
  Geographic Location: Montana
  Dates: Middle 1800s
  Main Characters (race, sex, age, nationality)
    Pretty-Shield (Crow Indian, female, approx. early 20s)

SYNOPSIS:
Pretty-Shield, born in the 1830s, tells the story of her life and times to Frank Linderman, a trusted friend. Through her recollections and Linderman's queries, the accounts of Crow lifestyle, beliefs, family relationships, and tribal practices are told. The descriptions of the storyteller, Pretty-Shield, and the emotional associations to her life events give this book special meaning. Through this woman's recollections, the importance of family, childhood, courtship, and medicine dreams are seen from a female perspective.

ILLUSTRATIONS:
There are a few black-and-white sketches portraying Plains Indian life of the nineteenth century.

STRENGTHS OF BOOK:
Pretty-Shield's life story includes the memories of a life prior to the white people and how it changed afterwards. The story is told with empathy, humor, warmth, and the appropriate sadness and anger.

CONTENT FOR FURTHER DEVELOPMENT:
The time frame and location of this story must be emphasized in order to understand the lifestyles and events of the Crow Indians. The practice of multiple wives may need some explanation so as to differentiate past from present.

∞∞∞∞∞∞∞∞∞∞∞∞∞∞

BOOK TITLE: **SING DOWN THE MOON**
AUTHOR: Scott O'Dell
PUBLISHER: Houghton Mifflin Publishing Co., 1970
FICTION
ISBN: None

READABILITY LEVEL: BOR: 4.2/ FLE: 5.0/ FOG: 6.0/ FRY: 5.0
DESCRIPTORS:
   Geographic Location: Arizona and New Mexico
   Dates: 1863-65

Main Characters (race, sex, age, nationality)
   Bright Morning (Navajo Indian, female, 14 yrs. old)
   Tall Boy (Navajo Indian, male, approx. 16-18 yrs. old)

SYNOPSIS:
Bright Morning lives with her family and Navajo Tribe in
Canyon de Chelly, Arizona. She spends her days watching the
sheep graze as they are essential sources of wool and meat for
her clan. One day as Bright Morning is herding the sheep, she
and a friend are captured by some Spaniards who sell them as
slaves in a nearby town. Fortunately, after several months,
Bright Morning and two friends succeed in escaping and, with
the help of two young Navajo warriors, they return to their
homes. However, Tall Boy, one of the braves, permanently
injures his arm in the process, thus making him an undesirable
suitor for Bright Morning. When white soldiers bring a notice
demanding that the tribe leave Canyon de Chelly, the Indians
hide in the hills with the hopes that the soldiers will leave. But
when the soldiers destroy their homes and crops, the tribe is
forced to travel with thousands of other Navajo Indians over
300 miles until they reach Fort Sumner, New Mexico. The men,
having little to do, sit idly by while the women do what they can
to establish new homes. As Tall Boy becomes more adept at
using just one arm, his prospects as a husband for Bright
Morning increase and they are eventually married. When it
becomes dangerous for Tall Boy to remain near the soldiers, he
and Bright Morning travel back to Canyon de Chelly and settle
their family in a hidden valley.

ILLUSTRATIONS: None

STRENGTHS OF BOOK:
This story is told from a Native American viewpoint so that
when Bright Morning is sold as a slave and when the Navajos
are forced to leave their homes, little explanation as to "why" is
given. Because of this, the reader, just as the Indians must have
been, may be somewhat confused. Certain Indian rituals are
described (e.g., entry into womanhood, marriage, healing) and
conflicts between different Indian tribes are also presented,

dispelling the myth that all Indians are alike. This story is available as a filmstrip, spoken recording, and videorecording.

CONTENT FOR FURTHER DEVELOPMENT:
Despite the value of the story's being told from the Indians' point of view, the postscript at the close of the book does not give a satisfactory explanation as to why various things happen. Further research into "Spanish slavers" and "the long walk" may be desirable.

∞∞∞∞∞∞∞∞∞∞∞∞∞

BOOK TITLE: **WOMAN CHIEF**
AUTHOR: Rose Sobol
PUBLISHER: Dial Press, 1976
FICTION
ISBN: 0-80307-9655-Z

READABILITY LEVEL: BOR: 7.0/ FLE: 9.5/ FOG: 10.8/ FRY: 10.0
DESCRIPTORS:
Geographic Location: Upper Missouri River, near Fort
Laramie, WY
Dates: Approx. 1815-45
Main Characters (race, sex, age, nationality)
Lonesome Star (Crow Indian, female, 10 yrs. old)

SYNOPSIS:
As this book opens, Lonesome Star's tribe, the Gros Ventres of the Prairie, is raided by an enemy tribe, the Crows. The women and children are taken by the Crows to become members of their tribe. Lonesome Star is adopted by Sharp Knife and his family. Above all, Lonesome Star wishes to become a hunter and participate in raids. To her delight, Sharp Knife is very supportive of her desire. Lonesome Star becomes an excellent hunter, better than many of the men in the tribe, and she is eventually allowed to go on forays. Through hard work Lonesome Star succeeds in accomplishing the four coups, or tests, of courage necessary to become a chief, and she becomes the only female ever to have a regular place at the council meetings.

ILLUSTRATIONS: None

STRENGTHS OF BOOK:
This book is based on a true story and details the life of this most
remarkable Indian woman. In a culture dominated by men it
was quite a feat for Lonesome Star not only to become a warrior,
but also to be granted the right to participate in the men's
council gatherings and to earn the right to be a chief.

CONTENT FOR FURTHER DEVELOPMENT:
When she became Chief, Lonesome Star, in her capacity as the
tribe's ruler, "married" another woman and this concept will
need further analysis. What exactly did this ritual marriage
signify and why did Lonesome Star not take a male consort?

∞∞∞∞∞∞∞∞∞∞∞∞∞∞

BOOK TITLE: **WAHEENEE: AN INDIAN GIRL'S STORY**
AUTHOR: Waheenee, as told to Gilbert L. Wilson
PUBLISHER: University of Nebraska Press, 1981 (Orig. pub.:
          Webb Publishing Co., 1921)
ILLUSTRATOR: Frederick N. Wilson
NON-FICTION
ISBN: 0-8032-4718-4

READABILITY LEVEL: BOR: 5.4/ FLE: 6.0/ FOG: 7.0/ FRY: 6.0
DESCRIPTORS:
   Geographic Location: Knife River, ND
   Dates: 1839-early 1900s
   Main Characters (race, sex, age, nationality)
      Waheenee, or Buffalo-Bird Woman (Hidatsa Indian,
         female, approx. 5 yrs. old)
      Various members of her family, tribe, and friends

SYNOPSIS:
This is Waheenee's account of everyday life from childhood to
adulthood. The chapters on childhood games and home life will
be particularly interesting to young children. Descriptions of the
work of men, women and children will aid in understanding

the old way of life of the Northern Plains Indians. The Hidatsa Indians made their living equally by hunting and farming and so the descriptions of home life and work cover a wide range of activities that were typical of the late nineteenth and early twentieth centuries. The explanatory notes and glossary of Indian words will add information for upper elementary children. The last chapter, "After Fifty Years," must be read with children. In only one page, Waheenee poignantly and succinctly describes the differences between the old way of life and the new.

ILLUSTRATIONS:
Accurate black-and-white drawings portray the everyday events of the Hidatsa during the late 1800s and early 1900s.

STRENGTHS OF BOOK:
The first-hand sketches of Indian life as told by Waheenee are rich in detail, and also include the importance of the human relationships within families and among members of the tribe. Waheenee's life spans the transitions from pre-white contact to the early decades of the twentieth century.

CONTENT FOR FURTHER DEVELOPMENT:
The Hidatsa Indians were farmers as well as hunters. How prevalent was farming among the various Native American tribes in the United States?

∞∞∞∞∞∞∞∞∞∞∞∞

BOOK TITLE: **BUFFALO MOON**
AUTHOR: G. Clifton Wisler
PUBLISHER: Lodestar Books, 1984
FICTION
ISBN: 0-525-67146-3

READABILITY LEVEL: BOR: 6.0/ FLE: 7.5/ FOG: 9.8/ FRY: 8.0
DESCRIPTORS:
    Geographic Location: Brazos River Area, TX
    Dates: Prior to 1861

Main Characters (race, sex, age, nationality)
    Willie Delamer (white, male, 14 yrs. old, American)
    Red Wolf (Comanche Indian, male, approx. 15-16 yrs. old)

SYNOPSIS:
Willie Delamer runs away from home when his parents insist on sending him to school in New Orleans. He does not feel he needs that type of formal education in order to operate the family's large cattle ranch and he plans to prove himself in a different fashion. Willie meets up with a group of Comanches that his father has a "peace treaty" with and is accepted into the tribe. He participates in and observes the daily life, rituals, games, and hunts of the Comanches and proves himself worthy in their eyes. Because of his family's business, Willie will become the future peacemaker between the tribe and the white people. After six months of living with the Comanches, Willie returns home.

ILLUSTRATIONS: None

STRENGTHS OF BOOK:
The author addresses the problems of adapting to Indian life and then back to the white people's way of life. The detailed depiction of Comanche life gives the reader a real feel for Native American rituals and the Indian conduct of life. There is mutual concern between the whites and the Indians not to fight anymore, hence the annual peace meeting. This story will have great appeal for male readers.

CONTENT FOR FURTHER DEVELOPMENT:
The Indian spiritual rituals involving chanting, dancing, and singing were not explained thoroughly. Another topic for discussion might be the diverse, and sometimes incompatible, views that the Indians and whites had towards such things as land ownership, nature, and what constituted achieving "manhood."

∞∞∞∞∞∞∞∞∞∞∞∞∞∞

BOOK TITLE: **AMERICAN INDIAN STORIES**
AUTHOR: Zitkala-Sa (Gertrude Bonnin)
PUBLISHER: University of Nebraska Press, 1985 (Orig. pub.:
        Hayworth Publishing House, 1921)
NON-FICTION
ISBN: 0-8032-9902-8 (pbk.)

READABILITY LEVEL: BOR: 7.0/ FLE: 12.0/ FOG: 14+/ FRY: 10.0
DESCRIPTORS:
    Geographic Location: The Dakotas
    Dates: Approx. 1880-1900
    Main Characters (race, sex, age, nationality)
        Zitkala-Sa (Sioux Indian, female, approx. 5-6 yrs. old to
           early 20s)
        Various members of her family, tribe, and friends

SYNOPSIS:
The first three chapters of this book, which comprise about half
of this work, are autobiographical in nature. They recount the
lifestyle of the Yankton Band of the Sioux Indians beginning
with the author's childhood to becoming an Indian teacher.
Growing up during this transitional period, Zitkala-Sa relates
the losses and sadness brought about by the white people's
occupation of Indian lands. The remaining eleven chapters are
short stories dealing with Indian lore, belief systems, nature, and
bridging the gap between the white and Native American
cultures.

ILLUSTRATIONS: None

STRENGTHS OF BOOK:
This first-hand account of the break from the old Indian way of
life to the changes brought about by the influence of the white
people is told simply, but with noted bitterness at the painful
losses.

CONTENT FOR FURTHER DEVELOPMENT:
The mystical elements of the stories other than Chapters 1, 2, and 3 may be difficult for children to understand.

∞∞∞∞∞∞∞∞∞∞∞∞∞∞

American Southwest

BOOK TITLE: **A STRANGER AND AFRAID**
AUTHOR: Betty Baker
PUBLISHER: Macmillan Company, 1972
FICTION
ISBN: None

READABILITY LEVEL: BOR: 5.1/ FLE: 7.5/ FOG: 7.6/ FRY: 6.0
DESCRIPTORS:
   Geographic Location: American Southwest, including
      present-day Arizona, New Mexico, Texas, and Kansas
   Dates: Approx. 1540-41
   Main Characters (race, sex, age, nationality)
      Sopete (Wichita Indian, male, approx. 12 yrs. old)
      Kima (Pawnee Indian, male, approx. 15 yrs. old)
      Zabe (Wichita Indian, male, approx. 8 yrs. old)

SYNOPSIS:
This is a story about what might have been one of the first
encounters between the Spanish and the Indians of the United
States Southwest in the first half of the sixteenth century. The
author begins with a brief note about how the rumors of the
Seven Cities of Gold began, explaining the Spanish desire for
gold and silver. The story's main character is Sopete, a Wichita
Indian captured along with his younger brother, Zabe, in a raid
by the Cicuye Indians. Although treated well, Sopete is very
unhappy in his new life, but Zabe, being younger than Sopete,
begins to forget his own heritage as he grows to accept the
Cicuyen ways. The Cicuyens are a Pueblo people, living in

cramped quarters built into the rocks, and Sopete hates the climbing and feels trapped in the homes. His life changes the day the Spanish make contact with the Indians, bringing with them horses--a new experience for the Cicuyens who fear these huge beasts that seem like monsters. Sopete and Kima, a Pawnee who was captured in a raid, accompany the Spanish on a buffalo hunt, and later are taken as hostages when the Spanish find no gold in the Indian villages. Hearing tales of much gold, Francisco de Coronado leads an expedition into the American Southwest and, upon finding no gold there, he takes severe action in several cities, including Arenal and Moho.

ILLUSTRATIONS:
The author included a map as a frontispiece which is very helpful in tracing the characters' movements in the story.

STRENGTHS OF BOOK:
The subject matter is one of this book's greatest strengths because it deals with a topic not often found in children's literature. The author is well versed in Native American culture and details the everyday life of the Indians, including their ceremonies, beliefs, and farming methods.

CONTENT FOR FURTHER DEVELOPMENT:
An excellent follow-up study is the clash of the Spanish and Indian cultures, and the harsh treatment of the Indians by the Spanish. These early encounters help to explain the heavy Spanish influence in the American Southwest and a related discussion might include the Jesuit missionaries who later came to convert the Indians. The great diversity among Native American tribes is evidenced in the difficulties Sopete experienced in adjusting to Cicuyen practices after having been raised a Wichita.

∞∞∞∞∞∞∞∞∞∞∞∞∞

BOOK TITLE: **WALK THE WORLD'S RIM**
AUTHOR: Betty Baker
PUBLISHER: Harper & Row, 1965

FICTION
ISBN: None

READABILITY LEVEL: BOR: 5.6/ FLE: 6.0/ FOG: 8.2/ FRY: 6.0
DESCRIPTORS:
Geographic Location: Southwest United States and Mexico
Dates: Late 1530s-early 1540s
Main Characters (race, sex, age, nationality)
Chakoh (Avavare Indian, male, 14 yrs. old)
Esteban (black, male, approx. 30s, African)
Alvar Núñez Cabeza de Vaca (white, male, approx. 30s,
Spanish)

SYNOPSIS:
The story begins with the synopsis of a real event that occurred
in 1527 when five Spanish ships left Cuba to explore Florida and
only four men survived the ill-fated journey. There were three
Spaniards, Cabeza de Vaca, Dorantes, and Castillo Maldonado,
and Dorantes' black slave, Esteban. Taken for medicine men,
they are held captive for ten years and when they make their
escape, they take refuge with the Avavare Indian tribe near
present-day Galveston, Texas. The Chief's son, Chakoh, is very
taken with the "Men-from-the-Sun" and he becomes great
friends with Esteban. When the Spaniards leave for Mexico City,
Chakoh persuades his father to let him accompany them in
order to learn about the Spanish god and how to make more
food available to his people. On their trip to Mexico the five
men meet various Indian tribes, some friendly, some not. The
reader learns much about the early living conditions and
customs of the Southwest Indians. Once in Mexico City,
Chakoh's eyes are opened to a whole new world and he has
many adjustments to make. He is greatly distressed to discover
that Esteban is a slave, a type of person that Chakoh thinks has
no courage or honor. Eventually the two friends reconcile on a
trip to find the Seven Cities of Cíbola (Gold) and on this journey
Chakoh makes some important decisions.

ILLUSTRATIONS:
There is a very helpful map at the beginning of the book
detailing both the trips to Mexico City and the return journey.

STRENGTHS OF BOOK:
This book has realism and a basis in fact in its favor. One often forgets that the Spanish were in the southwest United States not long after Columbus' discovery of America and the reader glimpses in this story one of the first encounters between whites and Native Americans. Besides being an entertaining story, the book also contains some important moral lessons.

CONTENT FOR FURTHER DEVELOPMENT:
Among ideas for further discussion are: The reasons why the Spanish were in the United States; the Spanish practice of the enslavement of both Indians and Africans; the tremendous importance that the Indian culture placed on medicine men; and Chakoh's reactions to "civilization," for example, sleeping in a bed in a house, new foods, and wearing clothing. Was the white people's way of life better than the Indian's?

∞∞∞∞∞∞∞∞∞∞∞∞

BOOK TITLE: **BY CRUMBS, IT'S MINE!**
AUTHOR: Patricia Beatty
PUBLISHER: William Morrow & Co., 1976
ILLUSTRATOR: Front. by Loring Eutemey
FICTION
ISBN: 0-688-32062-7

READABILITY LEVEL: BOR: 4.1/ FLE: 5.0/ FOG: 7.8/ FRY: 5.0
DESCRIPTORS:
   Geographic Location: Arizona Territory
   Dates: 1882-83
   Main Characters (race, sex, age, nationality)
      Damaris Boyd (white, female, 13 yrs. old, American)
      William Boyd (white, male, approx. 11 yrs. old, American)
      Lucy Boyd (white, female, approx. 40 yrs. old, American)

SYNOPSIS:
As this story opens, the Boyd family--Father, Mother, and three children, Damaris, William, and Ann Viola--are traveling by

Pullman train from their home in St. Louis to the Arizona Territory where Mr. Boyd plans to resettle his family. Mr. Boyd's brother is already raising cattle there and the Boyds plan to join him. Not far from their destination, gold fever hits the train and all the men on board, including Mr. Boyd, head for the newly-discovered gold fields. Because of an odd turn of events, Damaris comes into possession of a collapsible hotel called the Nomad which has been traveling on a flat car on their train. The Boyds arrive in Leacock quite disoriented, soon making the acquaintance of old Mr. Ponder who drives them out to Owen Boyd's "cattle ranch." As it turns out, Owen is married to a white woman who was an Indian captive most of her life and so all her Apache relations are living in tipis on the Boyd ranch. This is all too much for Lucy Boyd who temporarily settles in Switzer Wells to await her husband's return. Under the guidance of their Aunt Willa, the Boyds set up the Nomad and go into business. Switzer Wells is going to be on the railroad line and the town becomes alive with railroad people, starting a boom.

ILLUSTRATIONS:
There is only one illustration--a frontispiece.

STRENGTHS OF BOOK:
This book differs from most other stories about the settlement of the West because of its humor. It would be an excellent choice for youngsters who are not avid readers because it is a funny tale that will appeal to both boys and girls. There are numerous Native Americans interacting with the whites and the book paints a vivid picture of life in a frontier town.

CONTENT FOR FURTHER DEVELOPMENT:
There are several phenomena mentioned in the book that could use further discussion including: dime novels, boom towns, gold fever, railroad construction, the relaxing of "standards" out West, and oddly enough, the curious anatomy of lizards.

∞∞∞∞∞∞∞∞∞∞∞∞∞

BOOK TITLE: **NAVAJO SLAVE**
AUTHOR: Lynne Gessner
PUBLISHER: Harvey House, 1976
FICTION
ISBN: 0-8178-5352-9

READABILITY LEVEL: BOR: 5.3/ FLE: 6.0/ FOG: 8.1/ FRY: 6.0
DESCRIPTORS:
   Geographic Location: Arizona and New Mexico
   Dates: Approx. 1850s
   Main Characters (race, sex, age, nationality)
      Straight Arrow, or Niño (Navajo Indian, male, 11 yrs. old)
      Tomás de Montilla (white, male, approx. 14 yrs. old,
         Mexican)
      Jake (white, male, approx. 40 yrs. old, American)

SYNOPSIS:
The story opens when Straight Arrow is eleven years old. He
and his father, Red Band, are Navajo Indians and while
attempting to scavenge for food, Red Band is killed and Straight
Arrow is captured by some Ute Indians. When the Utes sell him
to a Mexican slave trader, Straight Arrow begins a miserable and
painful journey to New Mexico where he is sold to a wealthy
Mexican landowner. Being a slave is anathema to Indians and
Straight Arrow, renamed Niño (meaning "boy" in Spanish), has
a most difficult time adjusting to his new life. While outwardly
he eventually assumes a docile and subservient demeanor,
inside he burns to escape and can think of nothing else. He is
assigned to work under Jake, an American who runs the stables.
Niño loves horses and this is the only part of his captivity in
which he can take joy. When Niño is given the task of teaching
Tomás, the *hacendado's* son, to ride, the two boys become covert
friends. Niño remains in captivity for over four years and the
book deals primarily with his life as a slave. There is a mystery
surrounding Jake and the *hacendado* that keeps the reader's
interest piqued throughout the entire book.

ILLUSTRATIONS:
Scattered throughout the text are many simple line drawings of
Indian motifs such as ears of corn, trees, plants, and abstract
designs.

STRENGTHS OF BOOK:
The story is very well written and presents a vivid portrayal of
the lives of Indians in captivity--a topic not often found in
children's literature. The conflict of cultures, in this case Indian
and Mexican, is evident in the differing perspectives on work,
religion, and daily living. This story will appeal to both boys and
girls.

CONTENT FOR FURTHER DEVELOPMENT:
This book points out the vast differences between the Indian
tribes of the American Southwest; for example, why were the
Utes selling other Indians into captivity? Stealing was acceptable
and normal behavior among Indians, but why was this not so in
white society? The whole issue of slavery will spark further
discussion about why humans sometimes value life so cheaply.

∞∞∞∞∞∞∞∞∞∞∞∞∞

BOOK TITLE: **WORDS BY HEART**
AUTHOR: Ouida Sebestyen
PUBLISHER: Little, Brown and Co., 1968
FICTION
ISBN: 0-316-77931-8

READABILITY LEVEL: BOR: 5.2/ FLE: 6.0/ FOG: 10.0/ FRY: 6.0
DESCRIPTORS:
  Geographic Location: Bethel Springs (in the American
    Southwest)
  Dates: 1910
  Main Characters (race, sex, age, nationality)
    Lena Sills (black, female, 11 yrs. old, American)
    Ben and Claudie Sills (black, approx. 30s, American)

SYNOPSIS:
This is a superbly-written book dealing with blacks in the American Southwest. The Sills family lives in an almost white town on a sharecropper farm. Eleven-year-old Lena does well in school and wins a Bible-verse memorization contest, defeating a local white boy who always wins. He respects her, but she is shunned by many of the townspeople. The family encounters problems with their neighboring sharecroppers and are threatened several times. When Ben, Lena's father, has to travel overnight to fix a fence and does not return, Lena goes in search of him and finds him injured, the victim of a hostile attack. She makes the attempt to get him home, but he dies on the way. Lena struggles with her feelings of hate and revenge, and with the non-violent way her father has taught her to deal with difficulties.

ILLUSTRATIONS: None

STRENGTHS OF BOOK:
This is an honest portrayal of a black girl in a small southwestern town and her endeavors to understand why she is different. Lena's father emerges as a very strong character who helps his daughter learn to deal with all kinds of people peacefully. The problems of being a sharecropper family and the attitudes of the townspeople are shown realistically. This book was produced as a "Wonderworks" episode in 1985 by the PBS Children's and Family Consortium, WQED Television, Pittsburgh, Pennsylvania.

CONTENT FOR FURTHER DEVELOPMENT:
The book has biblical leanings, because Ben Sills wanted to be a minister, and he draws a lot of his principles from the Bible. Religion is very important in black culture and this point might be further examined. The differences between sharecropping and proper land ownership should be investigated. Also worthy of discussion are the evidences of prejudice against the Sills family in a town that was predominantly white. It is very possible that many of the townspeople had never encountered

blacks before and, rather than forming their own opinions, they just "followed the crowd" in their attitudes towards the blacks.

∞∞∞∞∞∞∞∞∞∞∞∞∞∞∞

West Coast

GRADES K-3

BOOK TITLE: **THE BELL RINGER AND THE PIRATES**
AUTHOR: Eleanor Coerr
PUBLISHER: Harper & Row, 1983 (An I Can Read Book)
ILLUSTRATOR: Joan Sandin
FICTION
ISBN: 0-06-021354-X

READABILITY LEVEL: BOR: 3.3/ FLE: 3.5/ FOG: 4.5/ FRY: 1.5
DESCRIPTORS:
Geographic Location: California
Dates: 1818
Main Characters (race, sex, age, nationality)
Pio (Ahachmai Indian, male, approx. 8 yrs. old)
Old Carlos (Ahachmai Indian, male, approx. 60 yrs. old)
Padre Barona (white, male, approx. 40 yrs. old, Spanish)

SYNOPSIS:
Pio is a young Indian of the Ahachmai tribe living in the San
Juan Capistrano Mission in the early 1800s. Pio attends school
and has daily chores to attend to in the Mission, including
herding the sheep. Pio is not himself, however, because there
are rumors that pirates might attack the Mission and all day long
he thinks about learning how to ring the Mission bells in order
to warn his family and friends should this dreaded event take
place. It is a great honor to be permitted to ring the bells and
Pio's concern and persistence eventually pay off when the
pirates, led by General Bouchard, do indeed attack the Mission.

ILLUSTRATIONS:
Pleasant color illustrations fill the pages of this book, carefully following the plot. Young readers will enjoy seeing how the Indian children in this story filled their days.

STRENGTHS OF BOOK:
This book is based on real-life stories of the San Juan Capistrano Mission in California. The Mission was founded by Father Junípero Serra in 1776 and in December 1818 it was looted by General Hypolite Bouchard and his band of pirates. This is a good introduction for younger readers to the events taking place on the Pacific coast of the United States in the early years of the nineteenth century.

CONTENT FOR FURTHER DEVELOPMENT:
The founding of missions by the Spanish in the American Southwest and California and the part played by Spanish culture in the United States are two topics worthy of additional study. Children might enjoy looking at a map of California and noting the many Spanish names of the cities such as San Francisco, Los Angeles, and San Juan Obispo, and locating the San Juan Capistrano Mission which can be visited today.

∞∞∞∞∞∞∞∞∞∞∞∞∞∞

GRADES 4-9

BOOK TITLE: **THE BAD BELL OF SAN SALVADOR**
AUTHOR: Patricia Beatty
PUBLISHER: William Morrow and Co., 1973
ILLUSTRATOR: Front. by Ben F. Stahl
FICTION
ISBN: None

READABILITY LEVEL: BOR: 6.9/ FLE: 9.5/ FOG: 12.8/ FRY: 10.0
DESCRIPTORS:
Geographic Location: Santa Fe, NM, to San Bernardino, CA
Dates: 1843-45
Main Characters (race, sex, age, nationality)
Jacinto Delacruz, or Spotted Wild Horse (Comanche
Indian, male, approx. 13 yrs. old)
Santos Gamboa (Comanche Indian, male, approx. 40 yrs.
old)
Teodoro Ramírez (half-white, half-Serrano Indian, male,
approx. 13 yrs. old, Mexican)

SYNOPSIS:
Jacinto, a teenaged Comanche youth, has been captured and lives
as a house servant to a wealthy Mexican family in Santa Fe. He
rebels against his subjugation and is hence handed over to
Gamboa to accompany him on his journeys to California.
Gamboa and his fellow travelers are *Genizaros*, or Indians who
have converted to Christianity. Father Anton, a priest from
Switzerland, endeavors to convert Jacinto who refuses to attend
Mass and whose only desire is to return to his Comanche tribe.
Jacinto is forced to go to California and once he arrives there, he
plans to steal a wild horse and make his escape. He makes
friends with a Mexican youth named Teodoro and together they
tame horses. Unfortunately, the two boys are caught by some
Ute Indians and Teodoro is killed. Jacinto and Teodoro's
grandfather decide to cast a bell for the church, but it is an
imperfect bell whose ring is not pure or sweet. They hang it
anyway and Jacinto uses it to warn the local settlers of an
impending flood. The story ends with Jacinto's being granted
permission to return to his Indian homeland, but Jacinto
chooses to stay, at least until the damaged village can be rebuilt.
Jacinto remains true to his Comanche gods and heritage and
Father Anton is finally able to understand and respect Jacinto's
beliefs.

ILLUSTRATIONS:
A two-page map pictures Jacinto's journey from Santa Fe to
California.

STRENGTHS OF BOOK:
The story is loosely based on true settlement experiences in early California and the author includes a seven-page explanatory note.   Both Christian and Comanche religious beliefs are explored and the reader clearly understands the differences between the two.   Of special note is the detailed explanation of how the church bell was cast and hung.

CONTENT FOR FURTHER DEVELOPMENT:
The Ute Indians are portrayed as violent warriors and this tribe might be further studied, especially since they engaged in the enslavement of other Indians.   There are numerous violent occurrences in the book, for example, cockfighting, which was a very popular sport in the nineteenth century.   The book contains many foreign phrases, such as *Genizaro, raquero, bueno,* and *gracias,* and these words of Spanish origin may need explanation.

∞∞∞∞∞∞∞∞∞∞∞∞∞∞

BOOK TITLE: **EIGHT MULES FROM MONTEREY**
AUTHOR: Patricia Beatty
PUBLISHER: William Morrow and Co., 1982
FICTION
ISBN: 0-688-01047-4

READABILITY LEVEL: BOR: 4.9/ FLE: 6.0/ FOG: 7.7/ FRY: 6.0
DESCRIPTORS:
  Geographic Location: Monterey, CA
  Dates: 1916
  Main Characters (race, sex, age, nationality)
    Fayette Ashmore (white, female, 13 yrs. old, American)
    Lettie Ashmore (white, female, late 30s, American)
    Eubie Ashmore (white, male, 10 yrs. old, American)

SYNOPSIS:
The summer following her year in the eighth grade, Fayette's mother completes her librarianship training at the local library. Not long after, the library receives a letter from some women in

a mountain town requesting that books be sent to their town. Lettie Ashmore, a widow, volunteers for the job in the hopes that it will lead to a permanent position in the library. With great reluctance the library officials consent to her going, along with her two children. A muleteer, or mule driver, is hired to handle the eight mules and one horse that are used to carry supplies, books, and people. After the first muleteer injures himself, the Ashmores are forced to request the services of Mr. "Possum" Turlock, a man of questionable background but one very capable of driving the mule train. The Ashmores continue on their journey, creating library outposts wherever they find people willing to manage the books. They meet many different kinds of mountain people, moonshiners, and have many bouts with the mules during their adventure, but at the end the Ashmores have a greater self-confidence and are more aware of their capabilities.

ILLUSTRATIONS: None

STRENGTHS OF BOOK:
This novel is based on the journals of an actual librarian who went into the California mountains. The author's note at the end of the story helps to distinguish between fact and fiction in this tale. The characterizations are well-drawn and all occurrences are carefully explained.

CONTENT FOR FURTHER DEVELOPMENT:
The educational and service role of public libraries in America should be examined. Find out how many students frequent their local library on a regular basis.

∞∞∞∞∞∞∞∞∞∞∞∞∞∞

BOOK TITLE: **HAIL COLUMBIA**
AUTHOR: Patricia Beatty
PUBLISHER: William Morrow and Co., 1970
ILLUSTRATOR: Liz Dauber
FICTION
ISBN: None

READABILITY LEVEL: BOR: 4.0/ FLE: 6.0/ FOG: 7.2/ FRY: 5.0
DESCRIPTORS:
    Geographic Location: Astoria, OR
    Dates: 1893
    Main Characters (race, sex, age, nationality)
        Louisa Baines (white, female, 13 yrs. old, American)
        Columbia Baines (white, female, 42 yrs. old, American)
        Various members of the Baines and Pettigrew families

SYNOPSIS:
When Aunt Columbia comes to visit the Baines family in
Astoria, Oregon, she brings along many progressive ideas.
Unbeknownst to her family, Columbia married, but kept her
maiden name, had two children, and is now returning to her
home town as a widow. Her brother, the "Captain," is very
resistant to Columbia's new-fangled notions, thirteen-year-old
Louisa watches her aunt with awe and admiration, and timid
Mama is caught in the middle. An avid feminist and social
reformer, Aunt Columbia strives to help the minority groups in
the city, primarily the Finns and Chinese, and battles the corrupt
politicians in the city government. Her methods are somewhat
unorthodox, but they manage to get the tasks accomplished.
Louisa becomes Aunt Columbia's protégé, much to the Captain's
dismay, and the two women have many adventures together.
Ultimately, Aunt Columbia gains the respect and affection of the
entire Baines family.

ILLUSTRATIONS:
The half-page, black-and-white line drawings at the beginning of
each chapter accurately follow the story line.

STRENGTHS OF BOOK:
The book discusses female suffragettes, portraying them in a
positive and human light. The story also brings to light the
plight of immigrant groups, in this case, the Chinese and Finns.
As might be expected, Aunt Columbia is also an advocate of
temperance. The story's humor is an excellent way to introduce
readers not only to the beginnings of the women's rights

movement, but also to life in an Oregon town in the late nineteenth century.

CONTENT FOR FURTHER DEVELOPMENT:
Besides the suffrage movement, the little contact between Native Americans and whites might be discussed. Did the white people and Indians of the Northwest settle in towns together? The only Indian in the book is a rather slow, bodyguard type. The actual living conditions, problems, and job opportunities of immigrants in western towns is another point for development. The minorities in this book are somewhat stereotyped since they are not presented as individuals, and this may require additional discussion.

∞∞∞∞∞∞∞∞∞∞∞∞∞∞

Non-Fiction Enrichment Books

GRADES K-9

BOOK TITLE: **OVERLAND TO CALIFORNIA IN 1859: A GUIDE FOR WAGON TRAIN TRAVELERS**
AUTHOR: Compiled & Edited by Louis M. Bloch, Jr.
PUBLISHER: Bloch & Company, 1983
NON-FICTION
ISBN: 0-914276-03-4

READABILITY LEVEL: BOR: 7.8/ FLE: 12.0/ FOG: 14+/ FRY: 12.5
DESCRIPTORS:
Geographic Location: American West
Dates: 1859

SYNOPSIS:
The majority of this fascinating book consists of actual quotations taken from *The Prairie Traveler*, a handbook for overland expeditions written by Randolph B. Marcy, a captain in the United States Army, published in 1859. The volume is full of maps, illustrations, and advertisements from the era. The compiler, Louis Bloch, also includes excerpts from histories of the West written in the 1850s. This work is a storehouse of practical information, beginning with which route was the best one to get to California. Included, also, is information about the organization of wagon trains; the amount of supplies and provisions needed per person; camping information; what kinds of clothing to take; marching and the care of the animals; the Indians encountered on the trip; the Nebraska, Kansas and Utah territories; and the development of California, including the reasons for the rapid settlement of the area. The factual nature of the book, coupled with the logical divisions of its chapters,

lends itself beautifully to reading aloud to the class followed by discussion.

ILLUSTRATIONS:
The book contains a wealth of illustrations and maps from the period of the 1850s. Included are diagrams of camping furniture and advertisements for wagons, saddles, baked goods, and other essentials that wagon train travelers would have needed on their journey. The compiler also included some interesting views of California and San Francisco in the mid-nineteenth century.

STRENGTHS OF BOOK:
The book's most attractive feature is the clear manner in which the factual information is presented. Also significant is the feeling the reader gets for the times and the way in which the wagon train pioneers made their way across the country. The book could be used by students as a reference source to complete certain assignments, such as organizing a wagon train (including the number of wagons, oxen, supplies, food, route, and which Indian tribes would be encountered) for the student's own family.

CONTENT FOR FURTHER DEVELOPMENT:
There are many ideas for development including the white people's relations with the Native Americans and why some Indians were friendly and others were not; the reasons for the boom-town growth of California; and the many different types and nationalities of people who went West and the various reasons for their decisions to emigrate.

∞∞∞∞∞∞∞∞∞∞∞∞∞

BOOK TITLE: **CHILDREN OF THE WILD WEST**
AUTHOR: Russell Freedman
PUBLISHER: Houghton Mifflin, 1983
NON-FICTION
ISBN: 0-89919-143-6

READABILITY LEVEL: BOR: 6.9/ FLE: 8.5/ FOG: 10.9/ FRY: 9.0
DESCRIPTORS:
Geographic Location: American West
Dates: Approx. 1848-1900

SYNOPSIS:
This non-fiction book is a photographic essay of the settlement of the western United States from the mid-nineteenth century to the turn of the century. The photographs are authentic and are supplemented by an informative and easy-to-read text. The book begins with a brief chapter on frontier photography. As the author explains, it sometimes took the photographer over an hour to assemble his equipment and a group of people for a portrait. Regardless of the time involved, most pioneers gladly stopped along the way to pose because it might be the only time in their lives that they would be photographed. Among some of the chapter topics are: the various modes of travel on the trip West; settling down on the homestead; the different types of homes in the West; the Native Americans, including their interactions with the whites; frontier schools; building in the West, including the origins of towns; and games, parties, and celebrations, depicting the lighter side of the settlement of the West.

ILLUSTRATIONS:
The black-and-white archival photographs are excellent and portray men and women of all races and ages engaged in numerous activities on the prairie. Children, the specific focus of this work, are depicted in many ways, showing different emotions and clothing styles. A full-page, clear map of the western United States details the various routes taken by western settlers.

STRENGTHS OF BOOK:
The combination of photographic and textual material is superb. The writing is clear in its explanation of pioneer life in the West and the illustrations closely supplement the author's words. Mr. Freedman based much of his writing on pioneer recollections and diaries, giving the book historical accuracy and authenticity.

Besides being an excellent story for reading aloud, the inclusion of a thorough index makes this a suitable reference book.

CONTENT FOR FURTHER DEVELOPMENT:
Native Americans are mainly shown as they are learning to give up their Indian ways and customs in their adaptation to the white people's world. The process by which this took place should spark further discussion. What difficulties did the Indians encounter as the old ways blended with the new? A comparison between prairie education and the schools of today should prompt a lively dialogue.

∞∞∞∞∞∞∞∞∞∞∞∞∞∞

BOOK TITLE: **COWBOYS OF THE WILD WEST**
AUTHOR: Russell Freedman
PUBLISHER: Clarion Books/Houghton Mifflin Co., 1985
NON-FICTION
ISBN: 0-89919-301-3

READABILITY LEVEL: BOR: 7.6/ FLE: 9.5/ FOG: 13.6/ FRY: 10.0
DESCRIPTORS:
Geographic Location: Cattle Country, West of Mississippi River
Dates: Late 1800s-early 1900s
Main Characters (race, sex, age, nationality)
Cowboys: Anglos, Spanish, Black, Native American, Mexican

SYNOPSIS:
Commencing with a background history beginning in the 1600s with the Spanish haciendas, the content of this fascinating book details the real-life experiences of American cowboys. Their motivation to be cowboys helps to capture the foundations of the camaraderie among these often lonely young men. Their labors and working conditions are observed in the well-chosen photographs. The author explores many areas of the cowboy's existence, including his mode of recreation, salary, and living

expenses. Quotations from actual cowboys add richness and reality to this well-written account.

ILLUSTRATIONS:
The archival photographs capture the action, living conditions, and the setting of cowboy life and work.

STRENGTHS OF BOOK:
The photographs, quotations from cowboys, and the smooth writing style deal with real cowboys and with their role in the Old West. This book will probably appeal more to boys than girls and should be instrumental in dispelling many of the myths and misconceptions of Hollywood cowboys.

CONTENT FOR FURTHER DEVELOPMENT:
How do the cowboys in the book compare to cowboys portrayed in film and on television? Was being a cowboy an exciting and romantic lifestyle? What kinds of responsibilities did cowboys have?

∞∞∞∞∞∞∞∞∞∞∞∞∞

BOOK TITLE: **INDIAN CHIEFS**
AUTHOR: Russell Freedman
PUBLISHER: Holiday House, 1987
NON-FICTION
ISBN: 0-8234-0625-3

READABILITY LEVEL: BOR: 6.1/ FLE: 7.5/ FOG: 10.6/ FRY: 8.0
DESCRIPTORS:
   Geographic Location: Texas, Great Plains, and American
      Northwest
   Dates: 1850-90

SYNOPSIS:
As this book shows, the Native American tribes of the West were as different from each other as the many countries of Europe. Trouble began for the Indians when the white settlers began to claim Indian lands and the United States Army was assigned the task of protecting the whites. This book deals with

six Indian Chiefs and the choices they faced: should they accept the dictates from Washington, D.C. and try and secure as much land as possible for their people, or should they resist and make war for what they believed was rightfully theirs? The Indian leaders--Red Cloud of the Oglala Sioux, Satanata of the Kiowas, the Comanche Quanah Parker, Washakie of the Shoshoni, Joseph of the Nez Percé, and the Hunkpaga Sioux, Sitting Bull--handled this challenge in various ways. General Philip Sheridan summarized the situation in the following way: "We took away their country and means of support, broke up their mode of living, their habits of life, introduced disease and decay among them. And it was for this and against this that they made war. Could anyone expect less?" (p. 65). Accustomed to hunting, roving, and raiding, reservation life was anathema to Native Americans--a stifling, stagnant existence they simply could not comprehend or accept. The book concludes with the Battle of Wounded Knee Creek in 1890 which marked the end of the Indian wars in the American West.

ILLUSTRATIONS:
The author included a treasure-house of archival photographs, many of them full-page, of the Native American and white participants in the Indian wars. In addition, a detailed map and numerous artists' renditions of battle scenes, Indian living conditions, and the white people's stamp on the West enhance and support the text.

STRENGTHS OF BOOK:
The white people's treatment of the Indians in America is a sad and unjust story, and Mr. Freedman tells it with clarity and great compassion. Particularly poignant is the account of the fate of the Nez Percé Indians. The author has a flair for making non-fiction read like fast-paced adventure, thus making this book suitable for reading aloud. The book is well-researched, historically accurate, and presents both sides of the land issue. A bibliography and index are included.

CONTENT FOR FURTHER DEVELOPMENT:
There were some whites who championed Indian rights, such as General Oliver Otis Howard and Brigadier General Nelson Miles, and it would be interesting to find out if there were others in the nation who believed the government's policy was unfair. What part, if any, did the press play in this matter?

∞∞∞∞∞∞∞∞∞∞∞

BOOK TITLE: **LAURA INGALLS WILDER: GROWING UP IN THE LITTLE HOUSE**
AUTHOR: Patricia Reilly Giff
PUBLISHER: Viking Kestrel, 1987 (Women of Our Time Series)
ILLUSTRATOR: Eileen McKeating
NON-FICTION
ISBN: 0-670-81072-X

READABILITY LEVEL: BOR: 5.8/ FLE: 6.7/ FOG: 9.5/ FRY: 7.0
DESCRIPTORS:
Geographic Location: Great Plains
Dates: 1867-1957
Main Characters (race, sex, age, nationality)
Laura Ingalls Wilder (white, female, American)

SYNOPSIS:
It is 1930 when this book opens and Laura Ingalls Wilder is sixty-three years old. Living on her beloved Rocky Ridge Farm near Mansfield, Missouri, she is reminiscing about how hard life was when she was a child and how different the world of today is with its many conveniences. Laura did not begin to write her "Little House" books until she was in her sixties, although she was a regular contributor to farm magazines and the *Missouri Ruralist* newspaper. It was at the urging of her daughter, Rose (also a writer), that Laura began to put down into words the story of her life as a pioneer girl. Her first book, *Little House in the Big Woods* published in 1932, was as she phrased it, " . . . a labor of love, a memorial to my father" (p. 11). No one was more surprised than Laura at the success of her book and because of the constant letters from her young readers, she decided to write about her husband, Almanzo, and she titled this book *Farmer*

Boy. Laura then planned to write eight books, telling about her life as a homesteader and later as a farmer's wife. Laura spent the next twenty years of her life writing--whenever she could fit it in between all of her farm chores. She remained an active woman to the end of her days and she died just days after her ninetieth birthday in February 1957.

ILLUSTRATIONS:
The soft black-and-white drawings are scattered throughout the text and enhance the story through their depiction of Laura both as a little girl and as a mature woman. Children will clearly be able to distinguish between Laura the pioneer and Laura the author.

STRENGTHS OF THE BOOK:
Fans of the "Little House" books will delight in reading this biography of Laura Ingalls Wilder. It is very well written and it makes the story of Laura's life read like a great adventure story. But it was not always wonderful, and the author includes the difficult times in the the Wilders' lives, especially after they lost their crop to a sudden hailstorm. Like many others, Laura and Manly had to start all over again, but they did so with courage and spirit. The author does a splendid job of binding the two Lauras--the impish girl in the "Little House" books along with the real-life woman.

CONTENT FOR FURTHER DEVELOPMENT:
The tremendous amount of technological change during Laura's lifetime is an excellent topic for discussion. It is hard to imagine that Laura, who spent her early years in a soddy, in 1930 lived in a house with electricity, running water, a telephone, and a Chrysler in the garage! Technology also changed farming methods and the readers may want to investigate these changes in depth.

∞∞∞∞∞∞∞∞∞∞∞∞∞∞

BOOK TITLE: **NEBRASKA PIONEER COOKBOOK**
AUTHOR: Compiled by Kay Graber

PUBLISHER: University of Nebraska Press, 1974
ILLUSTRATOR: Peggy W. Link
NON-FICTION
ISBN: 0-8032-0945-2

READABILITY LEVEL:
DESCRIPTORS:
  Geographic Location: Nebraska Plains
  Dates: 1850-1900

SYNOPSIS:
This cookbook records recipes from the early pioneer days of the
sod-house period including immigrant cookery and cowboy fare.
Recipes are for foods often mentioned in pioneer accounts and
are described in much the same manner as they may have been
shared with neighbors in the past. While an experienced cook
will be able to follow the narrative recipes, children will have
difficulties with many of them. The real value of the recipes,
however, lies in describing the favorite foods of the Native
Americans, homesteaders, both American and foreign-born, and
the cowboys. Integrated with the recipes are selections from
books and manuscripts that describe the pioneer settings. Tips
on preserving food, home remedies, and household hints are
also included.

ILLUSTRATIONS:
Photographs and drawings show kitchens and utensils of the era.

STRENGTHS OF BOOK:
The inclusion of first-hand accounts from primary documents
enriches this cookbook. This book could be read aloud to
younger students, used in the later-elementary grades, or
utilized as a reference source.

CONTENT FOR FURTHER DEVELOPMENT:
Many of the recipes cannot be duplicated, but students may enjoy
making a "pioneer meal" using some of the simpler recipes.

∞∞∞∞∞∞∞∞∞∞∞∞∞∞

BOOK TITLE: **THE TRUE BOOK OF PIONEERS**
AUTHOR: Mabel Harmer
PUBLISHER: Children's Press, 1957
ILLUSTRATOR: Loran Wilford
NON-FICTION
ISBN: None

READABILITY LEVEL: BOR: 4.7/ FLE: 6.0/ FOG: 6.4/ FRY: 5.0
DESCRIPTORS:
    Geographic Location: The American West
    Dates: Approx. 1820s-80s

SYNOPSIS:
This book addresses the various aspects of pioneering including: where the pioneers originated; how they traveled; pioneer homesteads; food and clothing; the activities of pioneer children; how news traveled; and the coming of the railroads. The author clearly depicts how the settlers lived, including many details about their homes, such as how they were lit by candles, how soap was made, and the importance of the spinning wheel. Attention is also given to food and clothing--crops that were raised and then stored in cool cellars, how maple syrup was obtained, and how clothing was made from deerskin and wool. An important point is made that while the pioneers faced many dangers on their journey from hostile Indians, stampedes, or rugged terrain, the move west was also a very exciting experience and a chance for many of them to own land. Pioneer children had to work hard and had daily chores to attend to, but they still found time for play. The book closes with a chapter on the coming of the railroads and how this advancement affected the development of the West.

ILLUSTRATIONS:
The book's color and black-and-white illustrations are well-done and picture many of the events and objects the author is describing. A map of the West is included and many of the illustrations are full-page.

STRENGTHS OF BOOK:
One of the book's strengths is its reading level, lower-elementary, and 98% of the text is in words from the Combined Word List for Primary Reading. Although non-fiction, the book reads easily and will appeal to both sexes. The chapter divisions make this a good choice for reading aloud to classes.

CONTENT FOR FURTHER DEVELOPMENT:
The hard life of pioneer children might lend itself to more discussion, along with the development of the railroad and its impact on the West. The book only mentions Indians as a danger and children reading this book should be made aware that many Indians were friendly and of great help to the white settlers.

∞∞∞∞∞∞∞∞∞∞∞∞∞

BOOK TITLE: **IF YOU TRAVELED WEST IN A COVERED WAGON**
AUTHOR: Ellen Levine
PUBLISHER: Scholastic, Inc., 1986
ILLUSTRATOR: Charles Shaw
NON-FICTION
ISBN: 0-590-40153-X

READABILITY LEVEL: BOR: 5.0/ FLE: 6.0/ FOG: 8.3/ FRY: 6.0
DESCRIPTORS:
 Geographic Location: American West
 Dates: Middle 1800s

SYNOPSIS:
Written in a question-and-answer format, this book answers simple questions concerning travel in a covered wagon, such as: "What would your family bring in their covered wagon?", "Where would you sleep?", "What was the Oregon Territory?", and "What chores would you have to do?" The questions are answered in simple terms and speak to the child. Dates, landmarks, and names of travelers are used and make it very easy to relate to the present day. Another book of interest by

Ellen Levine is *If You Lived at the Time of the Great San Francisco Earthquake* (Scholastic, Inc., 1987).

ILLUSTRATIONS:
Brown pencil sketches on each page depict such scenes as crossing a river, Chimney Rock, and completing chores.

STRENGTHS OF BOOK:
Written very simply and clearly directed towards children, the questions are ones youngsters would be interested in knowing the answers to. The book would make an excellent resource for teachers, particularly for study unit ideas.

∞∞∞∞∞∞∞∞∞∞∞∞∞∞

BOOK TITLE: **THE STORY OF THE GOLDEN SPIKE**
AUTHOR: R. Conrad Stein
PUBLISHER: Children's Press, 1978 (Cornerstones of
                Freedom Series)
ILLUSTRATOR: Tom Dunnington
NON-FICTION
ISBN: 0-516-04621-7

READABILITY LEVEL: BOR: 7.2/ FLE: 9.5/ FOG: 9.8/ FRY: 10.0
DESCRIPTORS:
    Geographic Location: Nebraska to California
    Dates: Late 1850s-1869

SYNOPSIS:
In this book, the history of the joining of the Union Pacific and Central Pacific Railroads is presented in great detail. The author begins with an explanation of how railroad fever swept the nation and the importance of the railroad for both the transportation of people and goods. With the Union Pacific centered in the Great Plains and the Central Pacific in California, the stage was set for a great rivalry between the two companies that kept the country enthralled for over three years. Many Chinese worked for the Central Pacific and immigrants, primarily the Irish, labored for the Union Pacific. Indeed,

towards the end of the construction, ethnic rivalries were used to motivate the workers when their progress began to lag. The Union Pacific encountered Native American resistance to the coming of the "Iron Horses" and the author explains the reasons behind this. On the morning of May 10, 1869, the two railroads met at Promontory Point, Utah, and the whole nation celebrated as the last spike--the golden spike--was hammered into place.

ILLUSTRATIONS:
Gray, brown, white and black illustrations help young readers visualize the events taking place in the story. A map of the railway's route is included.

STRENGTHS OF BOOK:
The book is factually correct and makes the exciting history of the building of the transcontinental railroad come alive for its readers. Stein writes in a simple style for his intended audience.

CONTENT FOR FURTHER DEVELOPMENT:
The author makes some generalizations about the Irish that should be examined. Several of the more "uncivilized" elements of the West, such as boom towns, drinking, and gambling, are brought to light and these may need additional explanation. The recruitment and arrival of thousands of Chinese workers to the United States should spark some discussion; what problems did they encounter and how did they fare in their new country? Did Chinese families come too? People of legendary fame such as James Butler "Wild Bill" Hickok and William "Buffalo Bill" Cody are mentioned and children may want to learn about the real men behind the lore.

∞∞∞∞∞∞∞∞∞∞∞∞

BOOK TITLE: **THE STORY OF THE HOMESTEAD ACT**
AUTHOR: R. Conrad Stein
PUBLISHER: Children's Press, 1978 (Cornerstones of
            Freedom Series)
ILLUSTRATOR: Cathy Koenig
NON-FICTION
ISBN: 0-516-04616-0

READABILITY LEVEL: BOR: 6.4/ FLE: 4.2/ FOG: 10.6/ FRY: 7.5
DESCRIPTORS:
　　Geographic Location: Great Plains
　　Dates: 1862-1900

SYNOPSIS:
This non-fiction book presents a detailed explanation of the
Homestead Act of 1862 and its effects upon the development of
the West. It explains why the law was passed and provides
specific procedures needed to be followed in order to become a
homesteader. It discusses how the pioneers often lived in a
dugout until a cabin could be built. There were some advantages
to dugout living, primarily the cost, and one Nebraska settler
only paid $2.78 to construct his dugout. Farming on the Great
Plains is addressed by examining the use of John Deere's new
steel plow, and the ensuing strife between the farmers and
cattlemen.   Many of the problems that settlers faced are
mentioned, including the devastating grasshopper attack of 1874.
The author makes the people of the West seem real by giving
examples of how, besides working very hard, they also found
diversion in foot and horse races and in playing baseball.
Women are mentioned as the "real heroes of prairie settlement"
(p. 23).   The book concludes with a discussion of farming in the
West today.

ILLUSTRATIONS:
Three-color drawings are scattered throughout the book,
highlighting events in the text. No minority peoples are shown.
A map of the Great Plains would have been useful.

STRENGTHS OF BOOK:
The book presents a considerable amount of factual information
in an understandable fashion and gives young readers a clear
picture of pioneer life. This book is available as a spoken
recording.

CONTENT FOR FURTHER DEVELOPMENT:
Native Americans are only mentioned twice in the book. Once when the cattlemen use the threat of hostile Indians to scare away the homesteaders, and again when they are forced to leave their homes in Oklahoma. Women are portrayed quite realistically, but are not mentioned much. However, the author does state: "Their stability would give the frontier something it had never had--a recorded past" (p. 23-24). This statement could be a starting point for discussion about the role of women in the West.

∞∞∞∞∞∞∞∞∞∞∞∞∞∞

BOOK TITLE: **THE STORY OF THE OREGON TRAIL**
AUTHOR: R. Conrad Stein
PUBLISHER: Children's Press, 1984 (Cornerstones of Freedom Series)
ILLUSTRATOR: David J. Catrow
NON-FICTION:
ISBN: 0-516-04668-3

READABILITY LEVEL: BOR: 6.6/ FLE: 9.5/ FOG: 12.9/ FRY: 10.0
DESCRIPTORS:
   Geographic Location: Oregon Trail
   Dates: 1830s-40s

SYNOPSIS:
This non-fiction account presents for children the story of the Oregon Trail and its significance in American history. The book begins with the journey of missionaries Narcissa and Marcus Whitman who crossed the Oregon Trail in 1836 on their way to what is now Washington State. Included are quotations from Narcissa's journal detailing the everyday events of the trip which brings history to life for the reader. Although trappers and fur traders had been traversing the Oregon country since the beginning of the nineteenth century, it was not until the Whitman's journey that people were convinced that wagon trains and families could make the difficult crossing. The customary departure point was somewhere in Missouri and the 2,000-mile, six-month trip was one of the most grueling

overland journeys that Americans ever experienced. As one pioneer expressed it: "True they had suffered, but the satisfaction of deeds accomplished and difficulties overcome more than compensated and made the overland passage a thing never to be forgotten." (p. 31.)   The year 1843 marked the beginning of the mass movement to Oregon, partially in the effort to find good farmland, but also to help claim the area for the United States. Although the settlers feared Indian attacks, it was rampant disease, especially cholera, and the treacherous terrain that took the majority of white lives. The Oregon Trail was used heavily until around 1869 when the transcontinental railroad was completed and today visitors can still see the wagon ruts that mark the thousands of wagons that traveled over the Trail.

ILLUSTRATIONS:
The simple, three-color line drawings follow the story quite closely and will help children to picture the realities, both good and bad, of the journey west.

STRENGTHS OF BOOK:
This story is well-written and will appeal to both girls and boys. The factual information is presented in an interesting fashion, making the book read like an adventure story. The author's inclusion of quotations from the diaries and personal accounts of travelers such as Narcissa Whitman, Jesse Applegate, and Octavius Howe truly makes this "people's history" and introduces children to original historical sources.

CONTENT FOR FURTHER DEVELOPMENT:
Some of the landmarks along the 2,000-mile Trail are mentioned, for example, Fort Laramie, Independence Rock, and Fort Hall, and children will want to locate them on a map. The author mentions some mountain men who played a part in the early history of the Oregon country and children may want to learn more about these people. The subject of the ill-fated Donner party in 1846 and the cannibalism they engaged in will need special handling with younger readers. Discuss "Manifest Destiny" and why so many Americans were willing to make this

difficult trip to an untamed, unknown country. How would the children in the class feel if they had to make such a journey?

∞∞∞∞∞∞∞∞∞∞∞∞

BOOK TITLE: **THE LITTLE HOUSE COOKBOOK: FRONTIER FOODS FROM LAURA INGALLS WILDER'S CLASSIC STORIES**
AUTHOR: Barbara M. Walker
PUBLISHER: Harper & Row, 1979
ILLUSTRATOR: Garth Williams
NON-FICTION
ISBN: 0-06-026418-7

READABILITY LEVEL: BOR: 4.5/ FLE: 6.0/ FOG: 6.8/ FRY: 5.0
DESCRIPTORS:
    Geographic Location: Minnesota and the Dakotas
    Dates: 1870s-90s
    Main Characters (race, sex, age, nationality)
        The Charles Ingalls family and various neighbors

SYNOPSIS:
This cookbook identifies specific foods in the context of the various "Little House" books. Directions and recipes are given for the dishes as made by the Ingalls family, and how to make the same dish today. Thorough information is provided about the frontier foods gathered from the wilds, foods raised in gardens and from the farms, and the staples available from the country stores. The author explains why certain foods were plentiful or were considered to be special treats by the Ingalls. Through the carefully developed directions, children will be able to duplicate the frontier recipes with today's available foods and equipment.

ILLUSTRATIONS:
The original Garth Williams illustrations add the familiarity of the well-known "Little House" family and their friends and neighbors.

STRENGTHS OF BOOK:
The real value of this cookbook is the development of the background information about foods, in the nineteenth century and in the present day. Through this look at foods and eating customs, an important part of family life on the Great Plains is conveyed. With the updated recipes, readers will be able to duplicate the foods.

CONTENT FOR FURTHER DEVELOPMENT:
A comparison of cooking methods and foods of the nineteenth and twentieth centuries might be interesting. Do the children think they would like some of the dishes prepared by the Ingalls family? How does food reflect a particular culture's time, place, and values?

∞∞∞∞∞∞∞∞∞∞∞∞∞∞

BOOK TITLE: **THE TIPI: A CENTER OF NATIVE AMERICAN LIFE**
AUTHOR: David and Charlotte Yue
PUBLISHER: Alfred A. Knopf, Inc., 1984
ILLUSTRATOR: David Yue
NON-FICTION
ISBN: 0-394-96177-3

READABILITY LEVEL: BOR: 6.3/ FLE: 8.5/ FOG: 10.2/ FRY: 9.0
DESCRIPTORS:
   Geographic Location: Great Plains
   Dates: Prior to 1890s
   Main Characters (race, sex, age, nationality)
      Great Plains Indians

SYNOPSIS:
Through descriptions of the way of life of the Great Plains Indians of the nineteenth century and before, the role of the tipi as the center of family and tribal life is clearly defined. The tipi was a portable, comfortable, and beautiful dwelling for Indians as they traveled and when they camped for long periods of time. The use of special tipis such as the medicine lodge or burial

lodge are explained as are the appropriate customs related to the tipi. The decorations and furnishing are pictured.

ILLUSTRATIONS:
Through the text and the clear line drawings, the structure, decorations, and uses of the tipi are clearly depicted.

STRENGTHS OF THE BOOK:
While the text is simply told, the author conveys both the everyday utility of the tipi and its spiritual importance in terms that children will understand.

CONTENT FOR FURTHER DEVELOPMENT:
In the Afterword, "What Happened to the Tipis," the Plains Indians' dependence on the buffalo is briefly described. This interrelationship and the role of white people in slaughtering the buffalo needs further explanation. The present-day efforts of Native Americans to maintain their culture and traditions may also be examined.

∞∞∞∞∞∞∞∞∞∞∞∞

References

Adam, Kathryn. "Laura, Ma, Mary, Carrie, and Grace: Western Women as Portrayed by Laura Ingalls Wilder." In *The Women's West*, ed. by Susan Armitage and Elizabeth Jameson, 95-110. Norman : University of Oklahoma Press, 1987.

Adamson, Lynda C. *A Reference Guide to Historical Fiction for Children and Young Adults*. Westport, CT : Greenwood Press, 1987.

Allen, Raymond. "Jamie and Kit Collier: The Writer and the Historian." *Teaching Pre K-8* 18 (Jan. 1988) : 35-38.

"America's Cowboys: A History." *Cobblestone: The History Magazine for Young People* 3 (July 1982) : 1-48.

Bataille, Gretchen M. *American Indian Literature: A Selected Bibliography for Schools and Libraries*. Pomona, CA : National Association Interdisciplinary Ethnic Studies, Ethnic Studies Department, California State Polytechnic University, 1981.

Bataille, Gretchen M., and Kathleen Mullen Sands. *American Indian Women: Telling Their Lives*. Lincoln : University of Nebraska Press, 1984.

"The Best of the West." *The MAILBOX, the Idea Magazine for Teachers, Intermediate Edition* 8 (May/June 1986) : 19.

Blue, Rose. "History Through Fiction." *Teacher* 93 (Jan. 1976) : 50-52.

"Bonus Page: Charlotte's Web--How Do They Feel?" *Teaching Pre K-8* 18 (Feb. 1988) : 103.

Bruner, Katharine Everett. "Stereotypes in Juvenile Historical Fiction." *School Library Journal* 35 (Sept. 1988) : 124-125.

Byrnes, Deborah A. "Children and Prejudice." *Social Education* 52 (April/May, 1988) : 267-271.

"California: A State History." *Cobblestone: The History Magazine for Young People* 3 (May 1982) : 1-48.

California State Department of Education. Language Arts and Language Unit. *Recommended Readings in Literature, Kindergarten Through Grade Eight.* Sacramento : California State Department of Education, 1986.

Campbell, Joseph, with Bill Moyers. *The Power of Myth.* New York : Doubleday, 1988.

Carroll, Peter. "Teaching the New History: Thoughts for the 80s." *Learning 85* 14 (Oct. 1985) : 70-72.

Cianciolo, Patricia Jean, ed. *Picture Books for Children.* Chicago : American Library Association, 1973.

Cordier, Mary Hurlbut. "Prairie Schoolwomen, Mid-1850s to 1920s, in Iowa, Kansas, and Nebraska." *Great Plains Quarterly* 8 (Spring 1988) : 102-119.

District of Columbia Public Library. *The Afro-American in Books for Children: Including Books About Africa and the West Indies, A Selected List.* 3rd, rev. ed. Washington, D.C. : District of Columbia Public Library, Children's Service, 1985.

Eakin, Mary K., comp. *Good Books for Children: A Selection of Outstanding Children's Books Published 1950-65.* 3rd ed. Chicago : University of Chicago Press, 1966.

Fairbanks, Carol. *Prairie Women: Images in American and Canadian Fiction.* New Haven, CT : Yale University Press, 1986.

Gillespie, John T. *The Elementary School Paperback Collection.* Chicago : American Library Association, 1985.
_____. *The Junior High School Paperback Collection.* Chicago : American Library Association, 1985.

Gillespie, John T., and Christine B. Gilbert, eds. *Best Books for Children: Preschool Through the Middle Grades.* New York : R.R. Bowker Company, 1985.

Gillespie, Margaret C., and John W. Conner. *Creative Growth Through Literature for Children and Adolescents.* Columbus, OH : Charles E. Merrill, 1975.

Goble, Paul. *The Gift of the Sacred Dog.* Scarsdale, NY : Bradbury Press, 1980.
_____. *The Girl Who Loved Wild Horses.* Scarsdale, NY : Bradbury Press, 1978.

Gruber, Marcella, and Catherine Surdovel. "Using Children's Literature Across the Curriculum." *Learning 86* 15 (Sept. 1986) : 56-57.

Haviland, Virginia. *The Best of Children's Books, 1964-1978, Including 1979 Addenda.* New York : University Press Books, 1981.

Henke, Linda. "Beyond Basal Reading: A District's Commitment to Change." *The New Advocate* 1 ([Winter] 1988) : 42-51.

Highwater, Jamake. *The Ceremony of Innocence.* New York : Harper & Row, 1985.

_____. *I Wear the Morning Star.* New York : Harper & Row, 1986.

_____. *Legend Days.* New York : Harper & Row, 1984.

Hillerman, Tony. *The Boy Who Made Dragonfly: A Zuni Myth.* New York : Harper & Row, 1972; reprint, Albuquerque : University of New Mexico Press, 1986.

Howard, Elizabeth F. *America as Story: Historical Fiction for Secondary Schools.* Chicago : American Library Association, 1988.

Huck, Charlotte S., Susan Helper, and Janet Hickman. *Children's Literature in the Elementary School.* 4th ed. New York : Holt, Rinehart & Winston, 1987.

Hurst, Carol Otis. "Best of the West." *Teaching Pre K-8* 17 (Sept. 1987) : 107-108.

Identifying Sexism and Racism in Children's Books. Parts 1 and 2. New York : Council on Interracial Books for Children, 1978, sound filmstrip and teaching guide.

Kolb, Frances Arick. *Portraits of our Mothers.* Andover, MA : The Network, Inc., 1983.

Laughlin, Mildred Knight, and Letty S. Watt. *Developing Learning Skills Through Children's Literature: An Idea Book for K-5 Classrooms and Libraries.* Phoenix : Oryx Press, 1986.

Lima, Carolyn W. *A to Zoo: Subject Access to Children's Picture Books.* 2nd ed. New York : R.R. Bowker Company, 1986.

Lipson, Eden Ross. *The New York Times Parent's Guide to the Best Books for Children.* New York : Times Books, 1988.

Mahan, James M. "Less Stereotypic Portrayal of American Indians: A Needed Goal for Pre-Service and In-Service Teachers." *Teacher Educator* 20 (Winter 1984-1985) : 16-22.

Malcolmson, Anne. *Yankee Doodle's Cousins*. Boston : Houghton Mifflin, 1941; reprint, Boston : Houghton Mifflin, 1969.

McGowan, Thomas M. "Children's Fiction as a Source for Social Studies Skill-Building." *ERIC Digest* 37 (Mar. 1987) : [1-2]

Meehan, Betty-Jo. *The Old Pacific Northwest as Found in Children's Literature: A Bibliography*. Ashland, OR : Department of Library Science, Southern Oregon State College, 1976. ERIC, ED 132 062.

Michigan Department of State. History Division's Historical Museum and Lenawee County Historical Society. *The Homemade History Project*. Lansing : Michigan Department of State, 1980-81.

Monson, Dianne L., ed. *Adventuring with Books: A Booklist for Pre-K-Grade 6*. New ed. Urbana, IL : National Council of Teachers of English, 1985.

The New Columbia Encyclopedia, 1975 ed. S. v. "Black Hawk War" and "Waubeshiek."

"Notable 1987 Children's Trade Books in the Field of Social Studies." *Social Education* 52 (April/May 1988) : 312-319.

"Notable 1986 Children's Trade Books in the Field of Social Studies." *Social Education* 51 (April/May 1987) : 290-301.

"Notable 1985 Children's Trade Books in the Field of Social Studies." *Social Education* 50 (April/May 1986) : 294-302.

"Notable 1984 Children's Trade Books in the Field of Social Studies." *Social Education* 49 (April 1985) : 322-330.

"Now Make Your Classroom a Showplace of Creative Teaching!" Advertisement for *Macmillan Instant Activities Program*. *Instructor* 98 (Sept. 1988) : [75]

"The Oregon Trail." *Cobblestone: The History Magazine for Young People* 2 (Dec. 1981) : 1-48.

"Our Own Spanish Conquest, 1528-1605." *Cobblestone: The History Magazine for Young People* 2 (March 1981) : 1-[48].

Readability Index Program. Rel. [198?] Delta Software Company, [Ann Arbor, MI?]

Riley, Glenda. *Frontierswomen: The Iowa Experience.* Ames : Iowa State University Press, 1981.

Roney, R. Craig. "Multiethnicity in Children's Fiction." *Social Education* 50 (Oct. 1986) : 464-470.

Roucher, Nancy. "Observe a quiet dignity." *Instructor* 98 (Sept. 1988) : 58; and accompanying poster, "Strutting Pigeon, Wife of White Cloud, by George Caitlin." *Instructor* 98 (Sept. 1988) : [59-66]

Rudman, Masha Kabakow. *Children's Literature: An Issues Approach.* 2nd ed. New York : Longman, 1984.

Sadker, Myra Pollack, and David Miller Sadker. *Now Upon a Time: A Contemporary View of Children's Literature.* New York : Harper & Row, 1977.

Schlissel, Lillian, comp. *Women's Diaries of the Westward Journey.* New York : Schocken Books, 1982.

Schon, Isabel. *A Bicultural Heritage: Themes for the Exploration of Mexican-American Culture in Books for Children and Adolescents.* Metuchen, NJ : Scarecrow Press, 1978.
_____. *A Hispanic Heritage: A Guide to Juvenile Books About Hispanic People and Cultures.* Metuchen, NJ : Scarecrow Press, 1980.

"The Story of America's Buffalo." *Cobblestone: The History Magazine for Young People* 2 (August 1981): 1-48.

Stratton, Joanna L. *Pioneer Women: Voices from the Kansas Frontier*. New York : Simon & Schuster, 1981.

Sutherland, Zena. *The Best in Children's Books: The University of Chicago Guide to Children's Literature, 1973-1978*. Chicago : University of Chicago Press, 1980.
_____. *The Best in Children's Books: The University of Chicago Guide to Children's Literature, 1979-1984*. Chicago : University of Chicago Press, 1986.
_____. *History in Children's Books: An Annotated Bibliography for Schools and Libraries*. Brooklawn, NJ : McKinley Publishing Co., 1967.

Sutherland, Zena, and May Hill Arbuthnot. *Children's Books*. 7th ed. Glenview, IL : Scott, Foresman, 1986.

Sutherland, Zena, and Myra Cohn Livingston, eds. *The Scott, Foresman Anthology of Children's Literature*. Glenview, IL: Scott, Foresman, 1984.

Tetreault, Mary Kay Thompson. "Rethinking Women, Gender, and the Social Studies." *Social Education* 51 (March 1987) : 170-178.

Tiedt, Pamela L., and Iris M. Tiedt. *Multicultural Teaching: A Handbook of Activities, Information and Resources*. 2nd ed. Boston : Allyn and Bacon, 1986.

Timeliner. Rel. [1986] Tom Snyder Productions, Cambridge, MA.

Turner, Frederick Jackson. *Frontier and Section: Selected Essays of Frederick Jackson Turner*. Edited by Ray A. Billington. Englewood Cliffs, NJ : Prentice-Hall, 1961.

Uhreen, David. *Books for Children with Oregon Settings: A Revision of a Similar Booklist Compiled by the Jackson*

County Library System. Ashland, OR : Department of Library Science, Southern Oregon State College, 1976. ERIC, ED 132 063.

Unlearning Asian American Stereotypes. New York : Council on Interracial Books or Children, 1981, sound filmstrip and teaching guide.

Unlearning Chicano and Puerto Rican Stereotypes. New York : Council on Interracial Books for Children, 1982, sound filmstrip and teaching guide.

Unlearning "Indian" Stereotypes. New York : Council on Interracial Books for Children, 1978, sound filmstrip and teaching guide.

West, Elliott. "The Youngest Pioneers." *American Heritage* 37 (Dec. 1985) : 90-96.

Winkel, Lois, ed. *The Elementary School Library Collection: A Guide to Books and Other Media.* 15th ed. Williamsport, PA : Brodart Co., 1986.

Author/Title/Illustrator Index